C-4113 CAREER EXAMINATION SERIES

This is your
PASSBOOK for...

Associate Contract Specialist

Test Preparation Study Guide
Questions & Answers

COPYRIGHT NOTICE

This book is SOLELY intended for, is sold ONLY to, and its use is RESTRICTED to individual, bona fide applicants or candidates who qualify by virtue of having seriously filed applications for appropriate license, certificate, professional and/or promotional advancement, higher school matriculation, scholarship, or other legitimate requirements of education and/or governmental authorities.

This book is NOT intended for use, class instruction, tutoring, training, duplication, copying, reprinting, excerption, or adaptation, etc., by:

1) Other publishers
2) Proprietors and/or Instructors of "Coaching" and/or Preparatory Courses
3) Personnel and/or Training Divisions of commercial, industrial, and governmental organizations
4) Schools, colleges, or universities and/or their departments and staffs, including teachers and other personnel
5) Testing Agencies or Bureaus
6) Study groups which seek by the purchase of a single volume to copy and/or duplicate and/or adapt this material for use by the group as a whole without having purchased individual volumes for each of the members of the group
7) Et al.

Such persons would be in violation of appropriate Federal and State statutes.

PROVISION OF LICENSING AGREEMENTS – Recognized educational, commercial, industrial, and governmental institutions and organizations, and others legitimately engaged in educational pursuits, including training, testing, and measurement activities, may address request for a licensing agreement to the copyright owners, who will determine whether, and under what conditions, including fees and charges, the materials in this book may be used them. In other words, a licensing facility exists for the legitimate use of the material in this book on other than an individual basis. However, it is asseverated and affirmed here that the material in this book CANNOT be used without the receipt of the express permission of such a licensing agreement from the Publishers. Inquiries re licensing should be addressed to the company, attention rights and permissions department.

All rights reserved, including the right of reproduction in whole or in part, in any form or by any means, electronic or mechanical, including photocopying, recording, or by any information storage and retrieval system, without permission in writing from the Publisher.

Copyright © 2024 by
National Learning Corporation

212 Michael Drive, Syosset, NY 11791
(516) 921-8888 • www.passbooks.com
E-mail: info@passbooks.com

PASSBOOK® SERIES

THE *PASSBOOK® SERIES* has been created to prepare applicants and candidates for the ultimate academic battlefield – the examination room.

At some time in our lives, each and every one of us may be required to take an examination – for validation, matriculation, admission, qualification, registration, certification, or licensure.

Based on the assumption that every applicant or candidate has met the basic formal educational standards, has taken the required number of courses, and read the necessary texts, the *PASSBOOK® SERIES* furnishes the one special preparation which may assure passing with confidence, instead of failing with insecurity. Examination questions – together with answers – are furnished as the basic vehicle for study so that the mysteries of the examination and its compounding difficulties may be eliminated or diminished by a sure method.

This book is meant to help you pass your examination provided that you qualify and are serious in your objective.

The entire field is reviewed through the huge store of content information which is succinctly presented through a provocative and challenging approach – the question-and-answer method.

A climate of success is established by furnishing the correct answers at the end of each test.

You soon learn to recognize types of questions, forms of questions, and patterns of questioning. You may even begin to anticipate expected outcomes.

You perceive that many questions are repeated or adapted so that you can gain acute insights, which may enable you to score many sure points.

You learn how to confront new questions, or types of questions, and to attack them confidently and work out the correct answers.

You note objectives and emphases, and recognize pitfalls and dangers, so that you may make positive educational adjustments.

Moreover, you are kept fully informed in relation to new concepts, methods, practices, and directions in the field.

You discover that you are actually taking the examination all the time: you are preparing for the examination by "taking" an examination, not by reading extraneous and/or supererogatory textbooks.

In short, this PASSBOOK®, used directedly, should be an important factor in helping you to pass your test.

ASSOCIATE CONTRACT SPECIALIST

DUTIES

Associate Contract Specialists under administrative supervision, with wide latitude for the exercise of independent judgment and decision making, perform complex professional/supervisory work involved in the development and management of contracts for social services programs. All Associate Contract Specialists perform related work.

SCOPE OF THE EXAMINATION

The multiple-choice test may include questions on principles of supervision including training and evaluation; developing and evaluating contract proposals; budget and fiscal monitoring; program monitoring and evaluation; ability to write reports and correspondence and keep records; contract development; knowledge of fiscal monitoring of contracts; knowledge of program monitoring of contracts; standards of proper employee ethical conduct, and other areas including written expression; management of personnel resources and analytical thinking.

HOW TO TAKE A TEST

I. YOU MUST PASS AN EXAMINATION

A. WHAT EVERY CANDIDATE SHOULD KNOW

Examination applicants often ask us for help in preparing for the written test. What can I study in advance? What kinds of questions will be asked? How will the test be given? How will the papers be graded?

As an applicant for a civil service examination, you may be wondering about some of these things. Our purpose here is to suggest effective methods of advance study and to describe civil service examinations.

Your chances for success on this examination can be increased if you know how to prepare. Those "pre-examination jitters" can be reduced if you know what to expect. You can even experience an adventure in good citizenship if you know why civil service exams are given.

B. WHY ARE CIVIL SERVICE EXAMINATIONS GIVEN?

Civil service examinations are important to you in two ways. As a citizen, you want public jobs filled by employees who know how to do their work. As a job seeker, you want a fair chance to compete for that job on an equal footing with other candidates. The best-known means of accomplishing this two-fold goal is the competitive examination.

Exams are widely publicized throughout the nation. They may be administered for jobs in federal, state, city, municipal, town or village governments or agencies.

Any citizen may apply, with some limitations, such as the age or residence of applicants. Your experience and education may be reviewed to see whether you meet the requirements for the particular examination. When these requirements exist, they are reasonable and applied consistently to all applicants. Thus, a competitive examination may cause you some uneasiness now, but it is your privilege and safeguard.

C. HOW ARE CIVIL SERVICE EXAMS DEVELOPED?

Examinations are carefully written by trained technicians who are specialists in the field known as "psychological measurement," in consultation with recognized authorities in the field of work that the test will cover. These experts recommend the subject matter areas or skills to be tested; only those knowledges or skills important to your success on the job are included. The most reliable books and source materials available are used as references. Together, the experts and technicians judge the difficulty level of the questions.

Test technicians know how to phrase questions so that the problem is clearly stated. Their ethics do not permit "trick" or "catch" questions. Questions may have been tried out on sample groups, or subjected to statistical analysis, to determine their usefulness.

Written tests are often used in combination with performance tests, ratings of training and experience, and oral interviews. All of these measures combine to form the best-known means of finding the right person for the right job.

II. HOW TO PASS THE WRITTEN TEST

A. NATURE OF THE EXAMINATION

To prepare intelligently for civil service examinations, you should know how they differ from school examinations you have taken. In school you were assigned certain definite pages to read or subjects to cover. The examination questions were quite detailed and usually emphasized memory. Civil service exams, on the other hand, try to discover your present ability to perform the duties of a position, plus your potentiality to learn these duties. In other words, a civil service exam attempts to predict how successful you will be. Questions cover such a broad area that they cannot be as minute and detailed as school exam questions.

In the public service similar kinds of work, or positions, are grouped together in one "class." This process is known as *position-classification*. All the positions in a class are paid according to the salary range for that class. One class title covers all of these positions, and they are all tested by the same examination.

B. FOUR BASIC STEPS

1) Study the announcement

How, then, can you know what subjects to study? Our best answer is: "Learn as much as possible about the class of positions for which you've applied." The exam will test the knowledge, skills and abilities needed to do the work.

Your most valuable source of information about the position you want is the official exam announcement. This announcement lists the training and experience qualifications. Check these standards and apply only if you come reasonably close to meeting them.

The brief description of the position in the examination announcement offers some clues to the subjects which will be tested. Think about the job itself. Review the duties in your mind. Can you perform them, or are there some in which you are rusty? Fill in the blank spots in your preparation.

Many jurisdictions preview the written test in the exam announcement by including a section called "Knowledge and Abilities Required," "Scope of the Examination," or some similar heading. Here you will find out specifically what fields will be tested.

2) Review your own background

Once you learn in general what the position is all about, and what you need to know to do the work, ask yourself which subjects you already know fairly well and which need improvement. You may wonder whether to concentrate on improving your strong areas or on building some background in your fields of weakness. When the announcement has specified "some knowledge" or "considerable knowledge," or has used adjectives like "beginning principles of..." or "advanced ... methods," you can get a clue as to the number and difficulty of questions to be asked in any given field. More questions, and hence broader coverage, would be included for those subjects which are more important in the work. Now weigh your strengths and weaknesses against the job requirements and prepare accordingly.

3) Determine the level of the position

Another way to tell how intensively you should prepare is to understand the level of the job for which you are applying. Is it the entering level? In other words, is this the position in which beginners in a field of work are hired? Or is it an intermediate or advanced level? Sometimes this is indicated by such words as "Junior" or "Senior" in the class title. Other jurisdictions use Roman numerals to designate the level – Clerk I, Clerk II, for example. The word "Supervisor" sometimes appears in the title. If the level is not indicated by the title, check the description of duties. Will you be working under very close supervision, or will you have responsibility for independent decisions in this work?

4) Choose appropriate study materials

Now that you know the subjects to be examined and the relative amount of each subject to be covered, you can choose suitable study materials. For beginning level jobs, or even advanced ones, if you have a pronounced weakness in some aspect of your training, read a modern, standard textbook in that field. Be sure it is up to date and has general coverage. Such books are normally available at your library, and the librarian will be glad to help you locate one. For entry-level positions, questions of appropriate difficulty are chosen – neither highly advanced questions, nor those too simple. Such questions require careful thought but not advanced training.

If the position for which you are applying is technical or advanced, you will read more advanced, specialized material. If you are already familiar with the basic principles of your field, elementary textbooks would waste your time. Concentrate on advanced textbooks and technical periodicals. Think through the concepts and review difficult problems in your field.

These are all general sources. You can get more ideas on your own initiative, following these leads. For example, training manuals and publications of the government agency which employs workers in your field can be useful, particularly for technical and professional positions. A letter or visit to the government department involved may result in more specific study suggestions, and certainly will provide you with a more definite idea of the exact nature of the position you are seeking.

III. KINDS OF TESTS

Tests are used for purposes other than measuring knowledge and ability to perform specified duties. For some positions, it is equally important to test ability to make adjustments to new situations or to profit from training. In others, basic mental abilities not dependent on information are essential. Questions which test these things may not appear as pertinent to the duties of the position as those which test for knowledge and information. Yet they are often highly important parts of a fair examination. For very general questions, it is almost impossible to help you direct your study efforts. What we can do is to point out some of the more common of these general abilities needed in public service positions and describe some typical questions.

1) General information

Broad, general information has been found useful for predicting job success in some kinds of work. This is tested in a variety of ways, from vocabulary lists to questions about current events. Basic background in some field of work, such as sociology or economics, may be sampled in a group of questions. Often these are principles which have become familiar to most persons through exposure rather than through formal training. It is difficult to advise you how to study for these questions; being alert to the world around you is our best suggestion.

2) Verbal ability

An example of an ability needed in many positions is verbal or language ability. Verbal ability is, in brief, the ability to use and understand words. Vocabulary and grammar tests are typical measures of this ability. Reading comprehension or paragraph interpretation questions are common in many kinds of civil service tests. You are given a paragraph of written material and asked to find its central meaning.

3) Numerical ability

Number skills can be tested by the familiar arithmetic problem, by checking paired lists of numbers to see which are alike and which are different, or by interpreting charts and graphs. In the latter test, a graph may be printed in the test booklet which you are asked to use as the basis for answering questions.

4) Observation

A popular test for law-enforcement positions is the observation test. A picture is shown to you for several minutes, then taken away. Questions about the picture test your ability to observe both details and larger elements.

5) Following directions

In many positions in the public service, the employee must be able to carry out written instructions dependably and accurately. You may be given a chart with several columns, each column listing a variety of information. The questions require you to carry out directions involving the information given in the chart.

6) Skills and aptitudes

Performance tests effectively measure some manual skills and aptitudes. When the skill is one in which you are trained, such as typing or shorthand, you can practice. These tests are often very much like those given in business school or high school courses. For many of the other skills and aptitudes, however, no short-time preparation can be made. Skills and abilities natural to you or that you have developed throughout your lifetime are being tested.

Many of the general questions just described provide all the data needed to answer the questions and ask you to use your reasoning ability to find the answers. Your best preparation for these tests, as well as for tests of facts and ideas, is to be at your physical and mental best. You, no doubt, have your own methods of getting into an exam-taking mood and keeping "in shape." The next section lists some ideas on this subject.

IV. KINDS OF QUESTIONS

Only rarely is the "essay" question, which you answer in narrative form, used in civil service tests. Civil service tests are usually of the short-answer type. Full instructions for answering these questions will be given to you at the examination. But in case this is your first experience with short-answer questions and separate answer sheets, here is what you need to know:

1) Multiple-choice Questions

Most popular of the short-answer questions is the "multiple choice" or "best answer" question. It can be used, for example, to test for factual knowledge, ability to solve problems or judgment in meeting situations found at work.

A multiple-choice question is normally one of three types—

- It can begin with an incomplete statement followed by several possible endings. You are to find the one ending which *best* completes the statement, although some of the others may not be entirely wrong.
- It can also be a complete statement in the form of a question which is answered by choosing one of the statements listed.

4

- It can be in the form of a problem – again you select the best answer.

Here is an example of a multiple-choice question with a discussion which should give you some clues as to the method for choosing the right answer:

When an employee has a complaint about his assignment, the action which will *best* help him overcome his difficulty is to
- A. discuss his difficulty with his coworkers
- B. take the problem to the head of the organization
- C. take the problem to the person who gave him the assignment
- D. say nothing to anyone about his complaint

In answering this question, you should study each of the choices to find which is best. Consider choice "A" – Certainly an employee may discuss his complaint with fellow employees, but no change or improvement can result, and the complaint remains unresolved. Choice "B" is a poor choice since the head of the organization probably does not know what assignment you have been given, and taking your problem to him is known as "going over the head" of the supervisor. The supervisor, or person who made the assignment, is the person who can clarify it or correct any injustice. Choice "C" is, therefore, correct. To say nothing, as in choice "D," is unwise. Supervisors have and interest in knowing the problems employees are facing, and the employee is seeking a solution to his problem.

2) True/False Questions

The "true/false" or "right/wrong" form of question is sometimes used. Here a complete statement is given. Your job is to decide whether the statement is right or wrong.

SAMPLE: A roaming cell-phone call to a nearby city costs less than a non-roaming call to a distant city.

This statement is wrong, or false, since roaming calls are more expensive.

This is not a complete list of all possible question forms, although most of the others are variations of these common types. You will always get complete directions for answering questions. Be sure you understand *how* to mark your answers – ask questions until you do.

V. RECORDING YOUR ANSWERS

Computer terminals are used more and more today for many different kinds of exams.

For an examination with very few applicants, you may be told to record your answers in the test booklet itself. Separate answer sheets are much more common. If this separate answer sheet is to be scored by machine – and this is often the case – it is highly important that you mark your answers correctly in order to get credit.

An electronic scoring machine is often used in civil service offices because of the speed with which papers can be scored. Machine-scored answer sheets must be marked with a pencil, which will be given to you. This pencil has a high graphite content which responds to the electronic scoring machine. As a matter of fact, stray dots may register as answers, so do not let your pencil rest on the answer sheet while you are pondering the correct answer. Also, if your pencil lead breaks or is otherwise defective, ask for another.

Since the answer sheet will be dropped in a slot in the scoring machine, be careful not to bend the corners or get the paper crumpled.

The answer sheet normally has five vertical columns of numbers, with 30 numbers to a column. These numbers correspond to the question numbers in your test booklet. After each number, going across the page are four or five pairs of dotted lines. These short dotted lines have small letters or numbers above them. The first two pairs may also have a "T" or "F" above the letters. This indicates that the first two pairs only are to be used if the questions are of the true-false type. If the questions are multiple choice, disregard the "T" and "F" and pay attention only to the small letters or numbers.

Answer your questions in the manner of the sample that follows:

32. The largest city in the United States is
    A. Washington, D.C.
    B. New York City
    C. Chicago
    D. Detroit
    E. San Francisco

1) Choose the answer you think is best. (New York City is the largest, so "B" is correct.)
2) Find the row of dotted lines numbered the same as the question you are answering. (Find row number 32)
3) Find the pair of dotted lines corresponding to the answer. (Find the pair of lines under the mark "B.")
4) Make a solid black mark between the dotted lines.

VI. BEFORE THE TEST

Common sense will help you find procedures to follow to get ready for an examination. Too many of us, however, overlook these sensible measures. Indeed, nervousness and fatigue have been found to be the most serious reasons why applicants fail to do their best on civil service tests. Here is a list of reminders:

- Begin your preparation early – Don't wait until the last minute to go scurrying around for books and materials or to find out what the position is all about.
- Prepare continuously – An hour a night for a week is better than an all-night cram session. This has been definitely established. What is more, a night a week for a month will return better dividends than crowding your study into a shorter period of time.
- Locate the place of the exam – You have been sent a notice telling you when and where to report for the examination. If the location is in a different town or otherwise unfamiliar to you, it would be well to inquire the best route and learn something about the building.
- Relax the night before the test – Allow your mind to rest. Do not study at all that night. Plan some mild recreation or diversion; then go to bed early and get a good night's sleep.
- Get up early enough to make a leisurely trip to the place for the test – This way unforeseen events, traffic snarls, unfamiliar buildings, etc. will not upset you.
- Dress comfortably – A written test is not a fashion show. You will be known by number and not by name, so wear something comfortable.

- Leave excess paraphernalia at home – Shopping bags and odd bundles will get in your way. You need bring only the items mentioned in the official notice you received; usually everything you need is provided. Do not bring reference books to the exam. They will only confuse those last minutes and be taken away from you when in the test room.
- Arrive somewhat ahead of time – If because of transportation schedules you must get there very early, bring a newspaper or magazine to take your mind off yourself while waiting.
- Locate the examination room – When you have found the proper room, you will be directed to the seat or part of the room where you will sit. Sometimes you are given a sheet of instructions to read while you are waiting. Do not fill out any forms until you are told to do so; just read them and be prepared.
- Relax and prepare to listen to the instructions
- If you have any physical problem that may keep you from doing your best, be sure to tell the test administrator. If you are sick or in poor health, you really cannot do your best on the exam. You can come back and take the test some other time.

VII. AT THE TEST

The day of the test is here and you have the test booklet in your hand. The temptation to get going is very strong. Caution! There is more to success than knowing the right answers. You must know how to identify your papers and understand variations in the type of short-answer question used in this particular examination. Follow these suggestions for maximum results from your efforts:

1) Cooperate with the monitor

The test administrator has a duty to create a situation in which you can be as much at ease as possible. He will give instructions, tell you when to begin, check to see that you are marking your answer sheet correctly, and so on. He is not there to guard you, although he will see that your competitors do not take unfair advantage. He wants to help you do your best.

2) Listen to all instructions

Don't jump the gun! Wait until you understand all directions. In most civil service tests you get more time than you need to answer the questions. So don't be in a hurry. Read each word of instructions until you clearly understand the meaning. Study the examples, listen to all announcements and follow directions. Ask questions if you do not understand what to do.

3) Identify your papers

Civil service exams are usually identified by number only. You will be assigned a number; you must not put your name on your test papers. Be sure to copy your number correctly. Since more than one exam may be given, copy your exact examination title.

4) Plan your time

Unless you are told that a test is a "speed" or "rate of work" test, speed itself is usually not important. Time enough to answer all the questions will be provided, but this does not mean that you have all day. An overall time limit has been set. Divide the total time (in minutes) by the number of questions to determine the approximate time you have for each question.

5) Do not linger over difficult questions

If you come across a difficult question, mark it with a paper clip (useful to have along) and come back to it when you have been through the booklet. One caution if you do this – be sure to skip a number on your answer sheet as well. Check often to be sure that you have not lost your place and that you are marking in the row numbered the same as the question you are answering.

6) Read the questions

Be sure you know what the question asks! Many capable people are unsuccessful because they failed to *read* the questions correctly.

7) Answer all questions

Unless you have been instructed that a penalty will be deducted for incorrect answers, it is better to guess than to omit a question.

8) Speed tests

It is often better NOT to guess on speed tests. It has been found that on timed tests people are tempted to spend the last few seconds before time is called in marking answers at random – without even reading them – in the hope of picking up a few extra points. To discourage this practice, the instructions may warn you that your score will be "corrected" for guessing. That is, a penalty will be applied. The incorrect answers will be deducted from the correct ones, or some other penalty formula will be used.

9) Review your answers

If you finish before time is called, go back to the questions you guessed or omitted to give them further thought. Review other answers if you have time.

10) Return your test materials

If you are ready to leave before others have finished or time is called, take ALL your materials to the monitor and leave quietly. Never take any test material with you. The monitor can discover whose papers are not complete, and taking a test booklet may be grounds for disqualification.

VIII. EXAMINATION TECHNIQUES

1) Read the general instructions carefully. These are usually printed on the first page of the exam booklet. As a rule, these instructions refer to the timing of the examination; the fact that you should not start work until the signal and must stop work at a signal, etc. If there are any *special* instructions, such as a choice of questions to be answered, make sure that you note this instruction carefully.

2) When you are ready to start work on the examination, that is as soon as the signal has been given, read the instructions to each question booklet, underline any key words or phrases, such as *least, best, outline, describe* and the like. In this way you will tend to answer as requested rather than discover on reviewing your paper that you *listed without describing*, that you selected the *worst* choice rather than the *best* choice, etc.

3) If the examination is of the objective or multiple-choice type – that is, each question will also give a series of possible answers: A, B, C or D, and you are called upon to select the best answer and write the letter next to that answer on your answer paper – it is advisable to start answering each question in turn. There may be anywhere from 50 to 100 such questions in the three or four hours allotted and you can see how much time would be taken if you read through all the questions before beginning to answer any. Furthermore, if you come across a question or group of questions which you know would be difficult to answer, it would undoubtedly affect your handling of all the other questions.

4) If the examination is of the essay type and contains but a few questions, it is a moot point as to whether you should read all the questions before starting to answer any one. Of course, if you are given a choice – say five out of seven and the like – then it is essential to read all the questions so you can eliminate the two that are most difficult. If, however, you are asked to answer all the questions, there may be danger in trying to answer the easiest one first because you may find that you will spend too much time on it. The best technique is to answer the first question, then proceed to the second, etc.

5) Time your answers. Before the exam begins, write down the time it started, then add the time allowed for the examination and write down the time it must be completed, then divide the time available somewhat as follows:
   - If 3-1/2 hours are allowed, that would be 210 minutes. If you have 80 objective-type questions, that would be an average of 2-1/2 minutes per question. Allow yourself no more than 2 minutes per question, or a total of 160 minutes, which will permit about 50 minutes to review.
   - If for the time allotment of 210 minutes there are 7 essay questions to answer, that would average about 30 minutes a question. Give yourself only 25 minutes per question so that you have about 35 minutes to review.

6) The most important instruction is to *read each question* and make sure you know what is wanted. The second most important instruction is to *time yourself properly* so that you answer every question. The third most important instruction is to *answer every question*. Guess if you have to but include something for each question. Remember that you will receive no credit for a blank and will probably receive some credit if you write something in answer to an essay question. If you guess a letter – say "B" for a multiple-choice question – you may have guessed right. If you leave a blank as an answer to a multiple-choice question, the examiners may respect your feelings but it will not add a point to your score. Some exams may penalize you for wrong answers, so in such cases *only*, you may not want to guess unless you have some basis for your answer.

7) Suggestions
   a. Objective-type questions
      1. Examine the question booklet for proper sequence of pages and questions
      2. Read all instructions carefully
      3. Skip any question which seems too difficult; return to it after all other questions have been answered
      4. Apportion your time properly; do not spend too much time on any single question or group of questions

5. Note and underline key words – *all, most, fewest, least, best, worst, same, opposite,* etc.
6. Pay particular attention to negatives
7. Note unusual option, e.g., unduly long, short, complex, different or similar in content to the body of the question
8. Observe the use of "hedging" words – *probably, may, most likely,* etc.
9. Make sure that your answer is put next to the same number as the question
10. Do not second-guess unless you have good reason to believe the second answer is definitely more correct
11. Cross out original answer if you decide another answer is more accurate; do not erase until you are ready to hand your paper in
12. Answer all questions; guess unless instructed otherwise
13. Leave time for review

b. Essay questions
1. Read each question carefully
2. Determine exactly what is wanted. Underline key words or phrases.
3. Decide on outline or paragraph answer
4. Include many different points and elements unless asked to develop any one or two points or elements
5. Show impartiality by giving pros and cons unless directed to select one side only
6. Make and write down any assumptions you find necessary to answer the questions
7. Watch your English, grammar, punctuation and choice of words
8. Time your answers; don't crowd material

8) Answering the essay question

Most essay questions can be answered by framing the specific response around several key words or ideas. Here are a few such key words or ideas:

M's: manpower, materials, methods, money, management
P's: purpose, program, policy, plan, procedure, practice, problems, pitfalls, personnel, public relations
    a. Six basic steps in handling problems:
        1. Preliminary plan and background development
        2. Collect information, data and facts
        3. Analyze and interpret information, data and facts
        4. Analyze and develop solutions as well as make recommendations
        5. Prepare report and sell recommendations
        6. Install recommendations and follow up effectiveness

    b. Pitfalls to avoid
        1. *Taking things for granted* – A statement of the situation does not necessarily imply that each of the elements is necessarily true; for example, a complaint may be invalid and biased so that all that can be taken for granted is that a complaint has been registered

2. *Considering only one side of a situation* – Wherever possible, indicate several alternatives and then point out the reasons you selected the best one
3. *Failing to indicate follow up* – Whenever your answer indicates action on your part, make certain that you will take proper follow-up action to see how successful your recommendations, procedures or actions turn out to be
4. *Taking too long in answering any single question* – Remember to time your answers properly

IX. AFTER THE TEST

Scoring procedures differ in detail among civil service jurisdictions although the general principles are the same. Whether the papers are hand-scored or graded by machine we have described, they are nearly always graded by number. That is, the person who marks the paper knows only the number – never the name – of the applicant. Not until all the papers have been graded will they be matched with names. If other tests, such as training and experience or oral interview ratings have been given, scores will be combined. Different parts of the examination usually have different weights. For example, the written test might count 60 percent of the final grade, and a rating of training and experience 40 percent. In many jurisdictions, veterans will have a certain number of points added to their grades.

After the final grade has been determined, the names are placed in grade order and an eligible list is established. There are various methods for resolving ties between those who get the same final grade – probably the most common is to place first the name of the person whose application was received first. Job offers are made from the eligible list in the order the names appear on it. You will be notified of your grade and your rank as soon as all these computations have been made. This will be done as rapidly as possible.

People who are found to meet the requirements in the announcement are called "eligibles." Their names are put on a list of eligible candidates. An eligible's chances of getting a job depend on how high he stands on this list and how fast agencies are filling jobs from the list.

When a job is to be filled from a list of eligibles, the agency asks for the names of people on the list of eligibles for that job. When the civil service commission receives this request, it sends to the agency the names of the three people highest on this list. Or, if the job to be filled has specialized requirements, the office sends the agency the names of the top three persons who meet these requirements from the general list.

The appointing officer makes a choice from among the three people whose names were sent to him. If the selected person accepts the appointment, the names of the others are put back on the list to be considered for future openings.

That is the rule in hiring from all kinds of eligible lists, whether they are for typist, carpenter, chemist, or something else. For every vacancy, the appointing officer has his choice of any one of the top three eligibles on the list. This explains why the person whose name is on top of the list sometimes does not get an appointment when some of the persons lower on the list do. If the appointing officer chooses the second or third eligible, the No. 1 eligible does not get a job at once, but stays on the list until he is appointed or the list is terminated.

X. HOW TO PASS THE INTERVIEW TEST

The examination for which you applied requires an oral interview test. You have already taken the written test and you are now being called for the interview test – the final part of the formal examination.

You may think that it is not possible to prepare for an interview test and that there are no procedures to follow during an interview. Our purpose is to point out some things you can do in advance that will help you and some good rules to follow and pitfalls to avoid while you are being interviewed.

What is an interview supposed to test?

The written examination is designed to test the technical knowledge and competence of the candidate; the oral is designed to evaluate intangible qualities, not readily measured otherwise, and to establish a list showing the relative fitness of each candidate – as measured against his competitors – for the position sought. Scoring is not on the basis of "right" and "wrong," but on a sliding scale of values ranging from "not passable" to "outstanding." As a matter of fact, it is possible to achieve a relatively low score without a single "incorrect" answer because of evident weakness in the qualities being measured.

Occasionally, an examination may consist entirely of an oral test – either an individual or a group oral. In such cases, information is sought concerning the technical knowledges and abilities of the candidate, since there has been no written examination for this purpose. More commonly, however, an oral test is used to supplement a written examination.

Who conducts interviews?

The composition of oral boards varies among different jurisdictions. In nearly all, a representative of the personnel department serves as chairman. One of the members of the board may be a representative of the department in which the candidate would work. In some cases, "outside experts" are used, and, frequently, a businessman or some other representative of the general public is asked to serve. Labor and management or other special groups may be represented. The aim is to secure the services of experts in the appropriate field.

However the board is composed, it is a good idea (and not at all improper or unethical) to ascertain in advance of the interview who the members are and what groups they represent. When you are introduced to them, you will have some idea of their backgrounds and interests, and at least you will not stutter and stammer over their names.

What should be done before the interview?

While knowledge about the board members is useful and takes some of the surprise element out of the interview, there is other preparation which is more substantive. It *is* possible to prepare for an oral interview – in several ways:

1) Keep a copy of your application and review it carefully before the interview

This may be the only document before the oral board, and the starting point of the interview. Know what education and experience you have listed there, and the sequence and dates of all of it. Sometimes the board will ask you to review the highlights of your experience for them; you should not have to hem and haw doing it.

2) Study the class specification and the examination announcement

Usually, the oral board has one or both of these to guide them. The qualities, characteristics or knowledges required by the position sought are stated in these documents. They offer valuable clues as to the nature of the oral interview. For example, if the job involves supervisory responsibilities, the announcement will usually indicate that knowledge of modern supervisory methods and the qualifications of the candidate as a supervisor will be tested. If so, you can expect such questions, frequently in the form of a hypothetical situation which you are expected to solve. NEVER go into an oral without knowledge of the duties and responsibilities of the job you seek.

3) Think through each qualification required

Try to visualize the kind of questions you would ask if you were a board member. How well could you answer them? Try especially to appraise your own knowledge and background in each area, *measured against the job sought*, and identify any areas in which you are weak. Be critical and realistic – do not flatter yourself.

4) Do some general reading in areas in which you feel you may be weak

For example, if the job involves supervision and your past experience has NOT, some general reading in supervisory methods and practices, particularly in the field of human relations, might be useful. Do NOT study agency procedures or detailed manuals. The oral board will be testing your understanding and capacity, not your memory.

5) Get a good night's sleep and watch your general health and mental attitude

You will want a clear head at the interview. Take care of a cold or any other minor ailment, and of course, no hangovers.

What should be done on the day of the interview?

Now comes the day of the interview itself. Give yourself plenty of time to get there. Plan to arrive somewhat ahead of the scheduled time, particularly if your appointment is in the fore part of the day. If a previous candidate fails to appear, the board might be ready for you a bit early. By early afternoon an oral board is almost invariably behind schedule if there are many candidates, and you may have to wait. Take along a book or magazine to read, or your application to review, but leave any extraneous material in the waiting room when you go in for your interview. In any event, relax and compose yourself.

The matter of dress is important. The board is forming impressions about you – from your experience, your manners, your attitude, and your appearance. Give your personal appearance careful attention. Dress your best, but not your flashiest. Choose conservative, appropriate clothing, and be sure it is immaculate. This is a business interview, and your appearance should indicate that you regard it as such. Besides, being well groomed and properly dressed will help boost your confidence.

Sooner or later, someone will call your name and escort you into the interview room. *This is it.* From here on you are on your own. It is too late for any more preparation. But remember, you asked for this opportunity to prove your fitness, and you are here because your request was granted.

What happens when you go in?

The usual sequence of events will be as follows: The clerk (who is often the board stenographer) will introduce you to the chairman of the oral board, who will introduce you to the other members of the board. Acknowledge the introductions before you sit down. Do not be surprised if you find a microphone facing you or a stenotypist sitting by. Oral interviews are usually recorded in the event of an appeal or other review.

Usually the chairman of the board will open the interview by reviewing the highlights of your education and work experience from your application – primarily for the benefit of the other members of the board, as well as to get the material into the record. Do not interrupt or comment unless there is an error or significant misinterpretation; if that is the case, do not hesitate. But do not quibble about insignificant matters. Also, he will usually ask you some question about your education, experience or your present job – partly to get you to start talking and to establish the interviewing "rapport." He may start the actual questioning, or turn it over to one of the other members. Frequently, each member undertakes the questioning on a particular area, one in which he is perhaps most competent, so you can expect each member to participate in the examination. Because time is limited, you may also expect some rather abrupt switches in the direction the questioning takes, so do not be upset by it. Normally, a board member will not pursue a single line of questioning unless he discovers a particular strength or weakness.

After each member has participated, the chairman will usually ask whether any member has any further questions, then will ask you if you have anything you wish to add. Unless you are expecting this question, it may floor you. Worse, it may start you off on an extended, extemporaneous speech. The board is not usually seeking more information. The question is principally to offer you a last opportunity to present further qualifications or to indicate that you have nothing to add. So, if you feel that a significant qualification or characteristic has been overlooked, it is proper to point it out in a sentence or so. Do not compliment the board on the thoroughness of their examination – they have been sketchy, and you know it. If you wish, merely say, "No thank you, I have nothing further to add." This is a point where you can "talk yourself out" of a good impression or fail to present an important bit of information. Remember, *you close the interview yourself.*

The chairman will then say, "That is all, Mr. _____, thank you." Do not be startled; the interview is over, and quicker than you think. Thank him, gather your belongings and take your leave. Save your sigh of relief for the other side of the door.

How to put your best foot forward
Throughout this entire process, you may feel that the board individually and collectively is trying to pierce your defenses, seek out your hidden weaknesses and embarrass and confuse you. Actually, this is not true. They are obliged to make an appraisal of your qualifications for the job you are seeking, and they want to see you in your best light. Remember, they must interview all candidates and a non-cooperative candidate may become a failure in spite of their best efforts to bring out his qualifications. Here are 15 suggestions that will help you:

1) Be natural – Keep your attitude confident, not cocky
If you are not confident that you can do the job, do not expect the board to be. Do not apologize for your weaknesses, try to bring out your strong points. The board is interested in a positive, not negative, presentation. Cockiness will antagonize any board member and make him wonder if you are covering up a weakness by a false show of strength.

2) Get comfortable, but don't lounge or sprawl
Sit erectly but not stiffly. A careless posture may lead the board to conclude that you are careless in other things, or at least that you are not impressed by the importance of the occasion. Either conclusion is natural, even if incorrect. Do not fuss with your clothing, a pencil or an ashtray. Your hands may occasionally be useful to emphasize a point; do not let them become a point of distraction.

3) Do not wisecrack or make small talk
This is a serious situation, and your attitude should show that you consider it as such. Further, the time of the board is limited – they do not want to waste it, and neither should you.

4) Do not exaggerate your experience or abilities

In the first place, from information in the application or other interviews and sources, the board may know more about you than you think. Secondly, you probably will not get away with it. An experienced board is rather adept at spotting such a situation, so do not take the chance.

5) If you know a board member, do not make a point of it, yet do not hide it

Certainly you are not fooling him, and probably not the other members of the board. Do not try to take advantage of your acquaintanceship – it will probably do you little good.

6) Do not dominate the interview

Let the board do that. They will give you the clues – do not assume that you have to do all the talking. Realize that the board has a number of questions to ask you, and do not try to take up all the interview time by showing off your extensive knowledge of the answer to the first one.

7) Be attentive

You only have 20 minutes or so, and you should keep your attention at its sharpest throughout. When a member is addressing a problem or question to you, give him your undivided attention. Address your reply principally to him, but do not exclude the other board members.

8) Do not interrupt

A board member may be stating a problem for you to analyze. He will ask you a question when the time comes. Let him state the problem, and wait for the question.

9) Make sure you understand the question

Do not try to answer until you are sure what the question is. If it is not clear, restate it in your own words or ask the board member to clarify it for you. However, do not haggle about minor elements.

10) Reply promptly but not hastily

A common entry on oral board rating sheets is "candidate responded readily," or "candidate hesitated in replies." Respond as promptly and quickly as you can, but do not jump to a hasty, ill-considered answer.

11) Do not be peremptory in your answers

A brief answer is proper – but do not fire your answer back. That is a losing game from your point of view. The board member can probably ask questions much faster than you can answer them.

12) Do not try to create the answer you think the board member wants

He is interested in what kind of mind you have and how it works – not in playing games. Furthermore, he can usually spot this practice and will actually grade you down on it.

13) Do not switch sides in your reply merely to agree with a board member

Frequently, a member will take a contrary position merely to draw you out and to see if you are willing and able to defend your point of view. Do not start a debate, yet do not surrender a good position. If a position is worth taking, it is worth defending.

14) Do not be afraid to admit an error in judgment if you are shown to be wrong

The board knows that you are forced to reply without any opportunity for careful consideration. Your answer may be demonstrably wrong. If so, admit it and get on with the interview.

15) Do not dwell at length on your present job

The opening question may relate to your present assignment. Answer the question but do not go into an extended discussion. You are being examined for a *new* job, not your present one. As a matter of fact, try to phrase ALL your answers in terms of the job for which you are being examined.

Basis of Rating

Probably you will forget most of these "do's" and "don'ts" when you walk into the oral interview room. Even remembering them all will not ensure you a passing grade. Perhaps you did not have the qualifications in the first place. But remembering them will help you to put your best foot forward, without treading on the toes of the board members.

Rumor and popular opinion to the contrary notwithstanding, an oral board wants you to make the best appearance possible. They know you are under pressure – but they also want to see how you respond to it as a guide to what your reaction would be under the pressures of the job you seek. They will be influenced by the degree of poise you display, the personal traits you show and the manner in which you respond.

ABOUT THIS BOOK

This book contains tests divided into Examination Sections. Go through each test, answering every question in the margin. We have also attached a sample answer sheet at the back of the book that can be removed and used. At the end of each test look at the answer key and check your answers. On the ones you got wrong, look at the right answer choice and learn. Do not fill in the answers first. Do not memorize the questions and answers, but understand the answer and principles involved. On your test, the questions will likely be different from the samples. Questions are changed and new ones added. If you understand these past questions you should have success with any changes that arise. Tests may consist of several types of questions. We have additional books on each subject should more study be advisable or necessary for you. Finally, the more you study, the better prepared you will be. This book is intended to be the last thing you study before you walk into the examination room. Prior study of relevant texts is also recommended. NLC publishes some of these in our Fundamental Series. Knowledge and good sense are important factors in passing your exam. Good luck also helps. So now study this Passbook, absorb the material contained within and take that knowledge into the examination. Then do your best to pass that exam.

EXAMINATION SECTION

EXAMINATION SECTION
TEST 1

DIRECTIONS: Each question or incomplete statement is followed by several suggested answers or completions. Select the one that BEST answers the question or completes the statement. *PRINT THE LETTER OF THE CORRECT ANSWER IN THE SPACE AT THE RIGHT.*

1. Under the terms of a government letter contract, the schedule for completion cannot exceed 180 days from the date of the letter contract or _____% of the contract performance, whichever occurs first.

    A. 20   B. 40   C. 60   D. 80

2. Each of the following is an example of a constructive change to a contract EXCEPT

    A. exceeding the number of inspections from once a month, as set forth in the contract, to once a week
    B. eliminating an entire building from an educational complex, causing a 12% reduction in contract price
    C. orally imposing a new standard on the type of wood that can be used in making an acoustical fence
    D. specifying a particular performance level for electric generators that proves unattainable, and then revising the performance level downward

3. All government purchase orders must be

    A. cost-plus-fixed-fee
    B. fixed-price with economic adjustment
    C. cost-plus-incentive-fee
    D. firm-fixed-price

4. What is the term for a person who holds the property of another for a specific purpose pursuant to an agreement between the parties?

    A. Trustee   B. Obligor   C. Bailee   D. Grantee

5. Under the Firm Bid Rule, contractors are typically prohibited from withdrawing bids for a period of _____ days from submission.

    A. 10   B. 30   C. 60   D. 90

6. What is the doctrine which holds that the written terms of an agreement may not be varied by prior oral agreements?
_____ rule.

    A. Text preeminence   B. Adhesion
    C. Parole evidence   D. Hard copy

7. Which of the following is a contracting instrument that allows the government to expedite the purchase of products when the specific products, quantities, and prices are not known at the time the agreement is reached?

2 (#1)

   A. Blanket purchase agreement (BPA)
   B. On-the-spot ordering
   C. Micro-purchasing
   D. Basic ordering agreement (BOA)

8. Which of the following government officials has the authority to enter into and direct contract performance with private contractors?   8._

      I. Administrative contracting officer (AGO)
     II. Procuring contracting officer (PCO)
    III. Contract specialist

The CORRECT answer is:

   A. I, II   B. II *only*   C. II, III   D. I, III

9. Under a cost-plus-incentive-fee contract, the contracting officer and the contractor negotiate the following terms: The target cost is $100,000. The target fee is $80,000. The maximum fee is $100,000. The minimum fee is $40,000. Which of the following fee adjustment formulas is to be used for this contract?   9._

   A. 20/80   B. 33/67   C. 50/50   D. 80/20

10. Currently, under the FAR, purchases greater than $2,500 but not greater than $100,000 made through simplified procedures must be reserved exclusively for small businesses   10._

   A. under any and all circumstances
   B. unless a larger supplier can be shown to exist in an area of labor surplus
   C. if two or more small businesses can submit competitive offers
   D. if only one small business submits a bid that is found to be responsible and responsive

11. Each of the following is a type of indefinite-delivery contract EXCEPT   11._

   A. indefinite-quantity   B. time-and-materials
   C. definite-quantity   D. requirements

12. The modification of a contract price, schedule or terms to compensate the contractor for government changes is described as an equitable   12._

   A. adjustment   B. supplement
   C. deviation   D. amendment

13. One of the unique aspects of government contracting typically exists in the unilateral provisions of the _____ clause.   13._

   A. inspection   B. suspension
   C. specifications   D. changes

14. After a contract is awarded, the agency contracting officers required to hold a debriefing within _____ days of anyrequest by an unsuccessful contractor.   14._

   A. 5   B. 10   C. 30   D. 60

15. Which of the following terms refers to the sharing of rights and liabilities among a group of parties collectively and individually?   15._

   A. Serial   B. Mutual and exclusive
   C. Joint and several   D. Sum and separate

3 (#1)

16. In establishing an effective program for compliance with government ethics rules, a contractor should FIRST

    A. appoint a compliance officer
    B. articulate a code of ethics
    C. establish internal review procedures
    D. establish a training program

16.____

17. Normally, for simplified acquisitions, the government

    A. makes advance payments
    B. makes partial payments
    C. makes progress payments
    D. provides no contract financing

17.____

18. In the Simplified Contract Format, which of the following items generally appears FIRST?

    A. Contract schedule
    B. Clauses
    C. Solicitation/contract form
    D. List of documents and attachments

18.____

19. The reasonable estimate of the damages that would result from a contractual breach by the parties, stipulated in the contract, is known as _____ damages.

    A. mitigated   B. executory
    C. liquidated   D. cancelled

19.____

20. What type of contract is generally used for complex services where the scope of work can be clearly defined but the quality of performance must be made by subjective evaluation?

    A. Cost-plus-incentive-fee   B. Cost-plus-award-fee
    C. Requirements   D. Cost-plus-fixed-fee

20.____

21. What is the term for a minor change made to the technical data package that is granted, on a one-time-only basis, to help the contractor in the performance of the contract?

    A. Adjustment   B. Amendment
    C. Improvement   D. Deviation

21.____

22. The only important exception to federal gift rules involving contractors and government employees is the rule that one may accept an unsolicited gift having a market value of $20 or less per occasion, provided the value of all gifts from one person does not exceed _____ in any calendar year.

    A. $50   B. $100   C. $200   D. $500

22.____

23. Legally, a(n) _____ is an offer by the government to pay a supplier the price it quoted if it performs according to given terms and conditions.

    A. request for proposal (RFP)
    B. purchase order
    C. statement of work (SOW)
    D. oral solicitation

23.____

4 (#1)

24. Which of the following terms is used to describe the relationship between the parties to a contract?   24.__

    A. Reformation   B. Covenant
    C. Privity   D. Surety

25. Which of the following is NOT a provision of the Federal Acquisition Streamlining Act?   25.__

    A. The drug-free workplace requirements apply to all contracts, regardless of price.
    B. A default clause must be included in all fixed-price contracts exceeding $25,000.
    C. All claims exceeding $50,000 must be certified.
    D. The records retention requirements apply to sealed-bid contracts exceeding $100,000.

KEY (CORRECT ANSWERS)

1.	B		11.	B
2.	B		12.	A
3.	D		13.	D
4.	C		14.	A
5.	C		15.	C
6.	C		16.	B
7.	D		17.	D
8.	B		18.	C
9.	D		19.	C
10.	C		20.	B

21.	D
22.	A
23.	B
24.	C
25.	A

TEST 2

DIRECTIONS: Each question or incomplete statement is followed by several suggested answers or completions. Select the one that BEST answers the question or completes the statement. *PRINT THE LETTER OF THE CORRECT ANSWER IN THE SPACE AT THE RIGHT.*

1. Which of the following is another term for a simplified specification?   1.____

   A. Statement of work
   C. Requirement
   B. Purchase description
   D. Product description

2. For offenses that show a lack of business integrity or honesty, a contractor may be debarred for up to _____ years (s).   2.____

   A. 1   B. 3   C. 5   D. 10

3. The Federal Acquisitions Regulation's (FAR) rules for record retention require that a contractor maintain payroll sheets and tax withholding statements for a particular contract for a period of at LEAST _____ year(s).   3.____

   A. one   B. two   C. four   D. five

4. What is the term for the petty cash fund used by a government agency to make purchases under $500?   4.____

   A. Imprest fund
   C. Nugatory fund
   B. Pool
   D. Impound

5. A written contract that contains all the terms and conditions of the parties' agreement is described as   5.____

   A. formal
   C. constructive
   B. irrevocable
   D. integrated

6. When the government and contractor can identify most but not all of the performance uncertainties for contracts with extended performance periods, which type of contract is generally most appropriate?   6.____

   A. Cost-plus-fixed-fee
   B. Fixed-price with economic price adjustment
   C. Cost-plus-incentive-fee
   D. Firm-fixed-price

7. Which of the following federal laws prohibits contractors from using appropriated funds to influence any government employee regarding the award or modification of any federal contract?
   The _____ Act.   7.____

   A. Competition in Contracting
   B. Davis-Bacon
   C. Byrd Amendment
   D. Anti-Kickback

5

2 (#2)

8. Which of the following constitutes the minimum acceptable purchase description in a government contract?

    A. Brand name or equal   B. To be determined
    C. Best and final   D. Compliant item

9. Which of the following types of contracts makes a contractor the *sole source* for specific products or services during the term of the contract?

    A. Labor hours   B. Indefinite-quantity
    C. Time-and-materials   D. Requirements

10. Each of the following sections is typically included in a statement of work (SOW) EXCEPT

    A. applicable documents
    B. scope
    C. quality assurance provisions
    D. requirements

11. Which of the following is a legal instrument that allows a contractor to proceed with the performance of a contract though the final agreement has not been reached with the government on the terms and conditions?

    A. Performance bond
    B. Letter contract
    C. Justification and approval
    D. First article

12. What is the term for the payment of money (or other thing of value) which is usually less than the amount owed or demanded, in exchange for extinguishment of a debt?

    A. Accord and satisfaction
    B. Demand waiver
    C. Compromise and settlement
    D. Rescission

13. Invoices for federal contract work are submitted on form

    A. DD1547   B. OF347   C. SF44   D. SF1411

14. Government workers who determine the supplies and services needed by the agency, their technical characteristics, and their quantities are known as

    A. contract specialists
    B. procurement contracting officers (PCOs)
    C. requirements people
    D. administrative contracting officers (ACOs)

15. Which of the following is NOT available to contractors who deliver services?

    A. On-the-spot purchases
    B. Fast payment procedures
    C. Micro-purchases
    D. Blanket purchase agreements

3 (#2)

16. The general etiquette of contract correspondence dictates that all correspondence be addressed   16.____

    A. first to the contracting officer, whether it directly concerns him/her or not, and then to the attention of others who are concerned (inspectors and contract specialists, etc.)
    B. only to the official from whom a response is required
    C. only to the contracting officer, who will then decide to whom the correspondence needs to be forwarded
    D. to the contracting officer and the highest-ranking officer within the department of the contracting agency

17. An Invitation for Bids is issued in the Simplified Contract Format (SCF). Which of the following sections will not become a physical part of the contract, but should be kept in the contract file?   17.____

    A. Contract schedule
    B. List of documents and attachments
    C. Representations and instructions
    D. Solicitation/contract form

18. Prompt payment provisions of the FAR require that an agency pay a proper invoice by the _____ calendar day after receipt by the billing office or after acceptance of the supplies or services.   18.____

    A. 5th   B. 10th   C. 30th   D. 60th

19. Sealed bidding is generally considered appropriate for government contracting if the   19.____

    A. award will be based on price and other price-related factors
    B. supply or service must be obtained from a sole source
    C. contractor must design a product
    D. government wants to consider alternative approaches to solving the problem

20. An obligation undertaken without consideration on behalf of another party is known as   20.____

    A. consignment   B. reconciliation
    C. accommodation   D. quid pro quo

21. Which of the following is a contractual instrument frequently used by government contracting officers to make repetitive purchases of $100,000 or less for the same or similar supplies or services?   21.____

    A. Fast payment procedure
    B. On-the-spot purchasing
    C. Option to extend
    D. Blanket purchase agreement

22. The civil penalties for contractors who violate the federal false claim statutes are a fine of between   22.____

    A. $1,000 and $5,000 per false claim
    B. $1,000 and $5,000 per false claim, plus twice the amount of loss sustained by the government
    C. $5,000 and $10,000 per false claim
    D. $5,000 and $10,000 per false claim, plus three times the amount of loss sustained by the government

4 (#2)

23. Which of the following must ALWAYS be included with a bid for a government contract?   23.__

    A. Descriptive literature
    B. A signed Certificate of Procurement Integrity
    C. A bid sample, if the contract is for a product
    D. A cover letter

24. Of the following sections in a government contract specification, which appears first?   24.__

    A. Quality assurance provisions
    B. Requirements
    C. Applicable documents
    D. Packaging

25. What is the term for a circumstance which must occur before an agreement becomes   25.__
effective, and which calls for the happening of some event before the contract is binding?

    A. Stipulation clause   B. Condition precedent
    C. Acceleration clause   D. Condition concurrent

KEY (CORRECT ANSWERS)

1.	B		11.	B
2.	B		12.	A
3.	C		13.	C
4.	A		14.	C
5.	D		15.	B
6.	B		16.	A
7.	C		17.	C
8.	A		18.	C
9.	D		19.	A
10.	C		20.	C

21.	D
22.	D
23.	B
24.	C
25.	B

EXAMINATION SECTION
TEST 1

DIRECTIONS: Each question or incomplete statement is followed by several suggested answers or completions. Select the one that BEST answers the question or completes the statement. *PRINT THE LETTER OF THE CORRECT ANSWER IN THE SPACE AT THE RIGHT.*

1. Which of the following systems of government contracting is prohibited by law?   1.____

    A. Indefinite-delivery
    B. Cost-plus-fixed-fee
    C. Labor-hour
    D. Cost-plus-percentage-of-cost

2. When there are government supplies _____ specifications, a warranty of specifications   2.____
   exists in a government contract.
       I. design
       II. procedural
       III. performance
   The CORRECT answer is:

    A. I only   B. I, II   C. II, III   D. I, III

3. Maximum penalties for contractors who violate the federal False Statements statutes   3.____
   include imprisonment for up to 5 years and a fine of up to _____ for each false statement.

    A. $10,000   B. $100,000   C. $250,000   D. $500,000

4. Changes that go beyond the scope of a contract are known as _____ changes.   4.____

    A. reconstructive   B. cardinal
    C. constructive   D. formal

5. In contract law, what is the term for something of value given in return for a performance   5.____
   or a promise of performance by another, for the purpose of forming a contract?

    A. Tender   B. Consideration
    C. Adhesion   D. Conveyance

6. Which of the following clauses is unique to government contracts?   6.____

    A. Partial termination
    B. No-cost termination
    C. Default
    D. Termination for convenience

7. In a typical contract arrangement, which of the following quality control systems are the   7.____
   government's responsibility, unless otherwise stipulated in the contract?
       I. Higher-level contract quality requirements for complex and critical items
       II. Standard inspection requirements for noncommercial items
       III. Commercial quality assurance systems for commercial items
   The CORRECT answer is:

    A. I only   B. I, II
    C. III only   D. None of the above

2 (#1)

8. In the federal acquisitions process, which of the following is typically performed FIRST?   8.__

    A. Purchase request   B. Statement of work
    C. CBD synopsis   D. Solicitation

9. Which of the following terms relates to the rights of a buyer to purchase the goods else-   9.__
where and hold the buyer responsible for the difference if the seller has breached a contract of sale?

    A. Cover   B. Puffing   C. form   D. Bailment

10. For most federal contract appeals involving claims of $50,000 or less, the agency to   10.__
whom the contractor should direct the appeal is the

    A. United States Claims Court
    B. General Services Administration Board of Appeals
    C. United States Court of Appeals for the Federal Circuit
    D. General Accounting Office

11. Each of the following is a guideline that should be followed in the contract inception   11.__
phase EXCEPT

    A. documenting all conversations with contracting officers and their representatives
    B. distributing different parts of the contract copy among the appropriate departments
    C. establishing company ethics codes and compliance programs
    D. never begin performance of the contract before receiving a signed copy of the con-
        tract award

12. Some contracts contain provisions establishing that upon the occurrence of a certain   12.__
event, such as a default in payments, a party's expired interest in the subject property will
become prematurely vested. This is a(n)

    A. anticipatory clause   B. stricture
    C. conveyance   D. acceleration clause

13. The government's policies and procedures travel by federal employees, defense materi-   13.__
als, public buildings and space, public utilities, and other programs and activities are usually found in the Federal

    A. Supply Service Regulations (FSSR)
    B. Acquisition Regulation (FAR)
    C. Property Management Regulations (FPMR)
    D. Information Resource Management Regulations (FIRMR)

14. Under a certain contract, the government has the unilateral right to exercise options for   14.__
additional duration. In order to exercise this option, the contracting officer must provide
the contractor with a preliminary written notice of intent to extend at least _____ days
before the contract expires.

    A. 10   B. 30   C. 60   D. 100

3 (#1)

15. Proposed procurements for _____ are listed in the COMMERCE BUSINESS DAILY (CBD).
      I.   perishable items
      II. $25,000 or more by federal agencies
      III. products made entirely from foreign sources
The CORRECT answer is:

    A. I *only*   B. II *only*   C. II, III   D. III *only*

16. In general, the method that is perceived as the most impartial for obtaining competitive bids in government contracting is

    A. competitive sealed negotiations
    B. two-step formal advertising and bidding
    C. competitive sealed bids
    D. request for proposals (RFP)

17. The *micro-purchase* threshold for government contracts is

    A. $500   B. $2,500   C. $5,000   D. $10,000

18. Under current bidding rules, a bid that arrives after the bid opening deadline is

    A. accepted if it is the lowest responsive bid
    B. accepted if it is postmarked on or before the bid opening deadline
    C. accepted if it is postmarked at least 5 days before the bid opening deadline
    D. rejected outright

19. Which of the following is/are forbidden by the Procurement Integrity Act?
      I.   Offering or giving any gratuity or thing of value to procurement officials under any and all circumstances
      II. Soliciting or obtaining from agency officials any proprietary or source selection information regarding a procurement
      III. Discussing future employment or business opportunities with procurement officials
The CORRECT answer is:

    A. I, II   B. II, III
    C. II *only*   D. I, II, III

20. Which of the following is most likely to be an authority of a government administrative contracting officer (ACO)?

    A. Reviewing progress payment requests
    B. Issuing change orders
    C. Changing contract specifications
    D. Altering the delivery schedule

21. Approximately what percentage of federal acquisitions are classified as *small purchases*?

    A. 10   B. 33   C. 75   D. 99

4 (#1)

22. The heart of any government contract is considered to be the 22._

    A. ordering agreement
    B. consideration
    C. financing method
    D. specification or statement of work

23. The most significant difference between a fixed-price and cost-reimbursement contract is the 23._

    A. term of the contract
    B. risk assumed by the contractor
    C. size of the contract
    D. types of goods or services

24. Which of the following terms is used to describe a contract which has not yet been fully completed or performed? 24._

    A. Anticipatory   B. Fiduciary
    C. Executory   D. Imperfect

25. The FAR requires that agencies which contract for commercial supplies and services use each of the following kinds of product descriptions, in a given order of preference. Which of the following types of product descriptions is preferred over the others? 25._

    A. Commercial item descriptions
    B. Voluntary standards
    C. Government design product descriptions
    D. Government functional and performance product descriptions

---

KEY (CORRECT ANSWERS)

1.	D		11.	B
2.	B		12.	D
3.	C		13.	C
4.	B		14.	C
5.	B		15.	B
6.	D		16.	C
7.	D		17.	B
8.	B		18.	C
9.	A		19.	B
10.	B		20.	A

21.	D
22.	D
23.	B
24.	C
25.	B

TEST 2

DIRECTIONS: Each question or incomplete statement is followed by several suggested answers or completions. Select the one that BEST answers the question or completes the statement. *PRINT THE LETTER OF THE CORRECT ANSWER IN THE SPACE AT THE RIGHT.*

1. Which of the following is a clause commonly found in construction contracts that protects the parties in the event that part of a contract cannot be performed due to causes beyond the control of the parties?

    A. Vis major   B. Executory clause
    C. Force majeure   D. Collapse clause

1.____

2. In the Uniform Contract Format (UCF) used in government contracting, Part III consists of

    A. the list of documents, exhibits, and other attachments
    B. contract clauses
    C. representations and instructions
    D. the schedule

2.____

3. Customarily, contract administrators maintain contract and solicitation files in _____ order.

    A. topical   B. alphabetical
    C. reverse chronological   D. forward chronological

3.____

4. The Walsh-Healey Public Contracts Act applies to most federal contracts over $10,000 that require the manufacture or furnishing of materials, supplies, articles, or equipment. Which of the following is subject to the provisions of this legislation?

    A. Newspapers, magazines, or periodicals
    B. Perishables
    C. Durable goods
    D. An item expressly authorized to be procured *in the open market*

4.____

5. Which of the following types of contracts is generally favored LEAST by the government?

    A. Cost-plus-fixed-fee
    B. Fixed-price with economic price adjustment
    C. Cost-plus-incentive-fee
    D. Firm-fixed-price

5.____

6. Which of the following would be an element of a contractor's solicitation file?

    A. Option letters   B. Abstracts
    C. Change orders   D. Internal working papers

6.____

7. From a contractor's point of view, the most desirable type of contract termination is the

    A. partial termination   B. no-cost termination
    C. default   D. termination for convenience

7.____

8. Generally, government construction contracts that exceed _____ contain Labor Standards Provisions for employment, wages, and hours.

    A. $1,000   B. $2,000   C. $5,000   D. $10,000

8.____

2 (#2)

9. A contractor requests an Invitation for Bids from a government agency. Later, the contractor receives a document that resembles a checklist, with only the titles of the clauses listed. The contractor should interpret this as a sign that

    A. the specifics of the IFB will be listed in the COMMERCE BUSINESS DAILY
    B. the bid opening process has already begun
    C. only one copy of the detailed IFB is available on the bid board at the regional office
    D. the IFB refers to a master solicitation that was not issued and must be requested

10. What is another term for an assignee?

    A. Trustee   B. Obligee   C. Grantee   D. Principal

11. An agency's Invitation for Bids (IFB) is issued in the Uniform Contract Format (UCF). In this format, the bidder enters its bid price under Section

    A. B, under the schedule
    B. H, under the schedule
    C. J, under the list of documents, exhibits, and other attachments
    D. L, under representations and instructions

12. Bid protests based on most things other than improprieties in a solicitation are generally required to be filed no later than

    A. before bid opening or the time set for initial proposals
    B. bid closing or the time when all proposals have been considered
    C. 10 days after the basis of the protest is known or shown to have been known
    D. 30 days after the basis of the protest is known or shown to have been known

13. When contracting with the federal government for construction services, all contracts in excess of _____ will require a bid bond under the law.

    A. $10,000   B. $25,000   C. $50,000   D. $100,000

14. In response to a *show cause* notice issued by the government, a contractor must

    A. demonstrate why its bid should be accepted over another nearly identical bid
    B. demonstrate why the contract should not be defaulted
    C. demonstrate the reasons why a progress payment is due
    D. cure a failure to perform the conditions of the contract

15. Under the incentive approach to value engineering change proposals, a contractor keeps _____% of the savings resulting from the approval of the change proposal if the contract is fixed-price.

    A. 25   B. 50   C. 75   D. 100

16. An important federal rule regarding contracting states that agencies may not spend, or commit themselves to spend, any monies before the funds have been appropriated. This rule is the

    A. Antideficiency Act
    B. necessary expense doctrine
    C. Acquisition Streamlining Act
    D. bona fide needs rule

3 (#2)

17. In general, bids submitted in response to government solicitations should include each of   17.____
the following EXCEPT

    A. required samples
    B. quantities
    C. a friendly letter outlining the firm's commitment
    D. a statement of credit

18. Which of the following occurs when a new party is substituted for another in a contract,   18.____
with the assent of all parties involved?

    A. Succession   B. Reciprocation
    C. Novation   D. Commutation

19. At the federal level, the most decentralized procurement process is conducted by the   19.____

    A. OMB   B. GSA
    C. civilian agencies   D. military

20. If it isn't a specific dollar amount, a typical bid bond is made for _____% of the total   20.____
amount of the bid.

    A. 5-10   B. 25-33   C. 50-75   D. 100

21. Which of the following general clauses is usually limited to construction contracts?   21.____

    A. Patents   B. Changed conditions
    C. Contingent fees   D. Inspection requirements

22. The Federal Acquisitions Regulation's (FAR) rules for record retention require that a con-   22.____
tractor maintain most financial and cost accounting records for a particular contract for a
period of at LEAST _____ year(s).

    A. one   B. two   C. four   D. five

23. Under most fixed-price with economic price adjustment contracts, the amount of increase   23.____
allowable is limited to _____% of the unit price.

    A. 5   B. 10   C. 15   D. 20

24. Which of the following methods of government contract financing is generally recom-   24.____
mended LEAST among both contractors and government contracting officials?

    A. Progress payments   B. Advance payments
    C. Partial payments   D. Assignment of claims

25. A bidder for a federal contract is required to submit a bid bond. Which form must be sub-   25.____
mitted to the agency?

    A. OF347   B. SBA1167   C. SF24   D. SF1402

4 (#2)

KEY (CORRECT ANSWERS)

1.	C		11.	A
2.	A		12.	C
3.	C		13.	B
4.	C		14.	B
5.	A		15.	B
6.	B		16.	A
7.	D		17.	C
8.	B		18.	C
9.	D		19.	C
10.	C		20.	A

21.	B
22.	C
23.	B
24.	B
25.	C

———

EXAMINATION SECTION
TEST 1

DIRECTIONS: Each question or incomplete statement is followed by several suggested answers or completions. Select the one that BEST answers the question or completes the statement. *PRINT THE LETTER OF THE CORRECT ANSWER IN THE SPACE AT THE RIGHT.*

1. Each of the following types of contracts is considered to be exempt from the government's Cost Accounting Standards (CAS) EXCEPT

    A. contracts and subcontracts for commercial items
    B. negotiated contracts and subcontracts of $500,000 or less
    C. negotiated cost-plus-fixed-fee contracts
    D. sealed-bid contracts

1.____

2. Typically, a pre-award survey (PAS) is requested when

    A. at least two firms have submitted bids that are nearly identical in their terms and pricing
    B. none of the bids submitted is determined to be both responsible and responsive
    C. the credit rating of a company is weaker than expected
    D. a company is the low bidder but other information is not available to make a determination of responsibility

2.____

3. The mandatory notice provisions of most contracts require that a contractor submit a formal stop work notice to the government within _____ days of the end of the period of work stoppage.

    A. 10   B. 20   C. 30   D. 40

3.____

4. Each of the following is typically the responsibility of a government contracting officer EXCEPT

    A. determining sizes, dimensions, and packaging requirements of supplies
    B. authoring a solicitation
    C. conducting the contracting process according to all applicable regulations
    D. legally obligating the government to pay for products or services

4.____

5. Government agencies typically use the sealed-bid process when

    A. the contract is an indefinite-delivery arrangement which will require constant communication with the chosen contractor
    B. the most important issue in the contract award is expected to be labor hours
    C. the aggregate value of the contract is $200,000 or less
    D. price will be the only basis for the award decision and there is no expectation that discussion with the offerors will be required

5.____

6. A contracting officer's warrant reads as follows: She is subject to FAR regulations and limited to supplies and services not to exceed $100,000. The organization listed is the Procurement and Contracts Division, and the agency is the Environmental Protection Agency. The contractor is aware that the officer was recently transferred from the Procurement and Contracts Division into the Office of Research and Development. Before entering into a contract with the officer, a contractor should

6.____

17

2 (#1)

A. wait to see an updated copy of the officer's Certificate of Appointment
B. contact the EPA head
C. make a photocopy of the old warrant and keep in on file
D. simply make sure the contract is less than $100,000, since the Office of R&D engages in contracting also

7. A contractual agreement to have the subject of a sale delivered to a designated place, usually either the place of shipment or the place of destination, without expense to the buyer, is described as

A. a specific performance
B. free on board
C. quantum meruit
D. a contract of bailment

8. Which of the following statements about no-cost contract settlements is/are TRUE?
I. The contractor keeps any money already paid as progress payments.
II. Each party agrees to walk away without any additional claim on the other.
III. The government pays all *kill* costs to subcontractors.
IV. The liability of each party is ended.
The CORRECT answer is:

A. I *only*
B. I, II, IV
C. II, IV
D. IV *only*

9. For a constructive suspension of work, a contractor is typically required to submit formal notice to the government within _____ days.

A. 10
B. 20
C. 30
D. 40

10. The most significant difference between an invitation for bids (IFB) and a request for proposals (RFP) is that an

A. RFP is more formal
B. RFP signals some uncertainty about the solicitation
C. IFB is more expensive for the contractor
D. IFB involves stricter rules for submission

11. When the government, through written or oral conduct, requires a contractor to make a change but does not specifically order it pursuant to the changes clause, a(n) _____ change has occurred,

A. interpretive
B. cardinal
C. constructive
D. informal

12. A contracting officer's cost analysis involves a direct evaluation of each of the following EXCEPT

A. the types of labor and corresponding number of hours
B. general and administrative expenses rate
C. the overall price of the contract
D. subcontracts

3 (#1)

13. Which of the following legal terms is used to describe a contract in which a dominant   13.____
party has taken unfair advantage of a weaker party?

    A. Adhesive   B. Unconscionable
    C. Quantum meruit   D. Unilateral

14. Information about federal purchases, including research and development, is available   14.____
directly through the

    A. Federal Systems Integration and Management Center (FED-SIM)
    B. Federal Procurement Data Center (FPDC)
    C. Procurement Automated Source System (PASS)
    D. National Technical Information Service (NTIS)

15. If a government contract is terminated for convenience, the contractor is required to sub-   15.____
mit a proposed termination settlement within

    A. 30 days   B. 90 days   C. 180 days   D. 1 year

16. An advance agreement is usually considered necessary when   16.____

    A. there is some doubt whether costs will be allowable
    B. costs are inconsistent with the established FAR principles
    C. the contract is cost-reimbursable
    D. costs are allocable

17. What is the term for the act of restoring a party to a contract to their status quo – i.e., the   17.____
position the party would have been in if no contract had been made?

    A. Remedy   B. Restitution
    C. Indemnification   D. Rescission

18. First article testing under government contracts is considered appropriate when   18.____

    A. the item is described by a performance specification
    B. the contract is for supplies covered by complete and detailed technical specifica-
       tions
    C. the contract is for supplies normally sold in the commercial market
    D. it is a research and development contract

19. Under the terms of the Buy American Act,   19.____

    A. the government may purchase services from foreign sources, but not goods
    B. only domestic products may be purchased for public use under most conditions
    C. only domestic products may be purchased for commissary resale
    D. the government cannot purchase foreign products under any circumstances

20. How many quotations (minimum) are required for a government contracting officer to   20.____
carry out a micro-purchase?

    A. 1   B. 2   C. 3   D. 4

4 (#1)

21. A company who submits a proposal in response to a government RFP is legally referred to as a(n) 21.___

    A. suitor B. bidder
    C. contestant D. offeror

22. The typical Option to Extend Services in a government contract permits the government to require continued performance 22.___

    A. for up to 6 months B. for up to 1 year
    C. for up to 3 years D. indefinitely

23. For most cost-plus-fixed-fee contracts, the maximum fee allowed by law is equal to _____% of the estimated cost of the contract. 23.___

    A. 5 B. 10 C. 15 D. 20

24. In an Invitation for Bids that is issued in the Uniform Contract Format (UCF), Federal Standard Form 33 includes each of the following EXCEPT 24.___

    A. a table of contents
    B. the time, date, and place where the bids will be opened
    C. a specification or statement of work
    D. the solicitation

25. Once the government is able to develop definite performance objectives that are probably achievable, but the probability is not high enough to warrant the use of a fixed-price contract, the contracting officer is most likely to draft a _____ contract. 25.___

    A. requirements B. cost-plus-incentive fee
    C. cost-plus-award-fee D. cost-plus-fixed-fee

KEY (CORRECT ANSWERS)

1.	C	11.	C
2.	D	12.	C
3.	C	13.	B
4.	A	14.	B
5.	D	15.	D
6.	A	16.	A
7.	B	17.	B
8.	B	18.	A
9.	B	19.	B
10.	B	20.	A

21.	D
22.	A
23.	B
24.	C
25.	B

TEST 2

DIRECTIONS: Each question or incomplete statement is followed by several suggested answers or completions. Select the one that BEST answers the question or completes the statement. *PRINT THE LETTER OF THE CORRECT ANSWER IN THE SPACE AT THE RIGHT.*

1. In contract law, a person having a legal duty, created by an undertaking, to act primarily for the benefit of another in matters connected with the undertaking, is a(n)

    A. fiduciary   B. obligor
    C. conservator   D. guardian

1.____

2. What percentage of all government purchases made through negotiation procedures are fixed-price?

    A. 40   B. 60   C. 80   D. 100

2.____

3. In documenting any claim, a contractor should include each of the following EXCEPT

    A. original solicitation documents
    B. an outline of extra or changed work forming the basis of the claim
    C. the legal basis or theory for the claim
    D. an explanation of the actual work performed

3.____

4. For offenses involving a violation of the Drug-Free Workplace Act, a contractor may be debarred for up to _____ year(s).

    A. 1   B. 3   C. 5   D. 10

4.____

5. Which of the following items of federal legislation serve to subject contractors to reviews and audits by the Department of Labor?
The
        I. Procurement Integrity Act
       II. Service Contract Act of 1965
     III. Davis-Bacon Act
     IV. Federal Acquisition Reform Act of 1996
The CORRECT answer is:

    A. I *only*   B. II, III
    C. III, IV   D. I, II, IV

5.____

6. If a contractor's response to an RFP includes a technical proposal, the proposal should be no longer than _____ pages under the rules.

    A. 10   B. 20   C. 50   D. 100

6.____

7. The federal agency which contracts for most common-use items and services throughout the government is the

    A. Office of Management and Budget (OMB)
    B. General Services Agency (GSA)
    C. General Accounting Office (GAO)
    D. Department of Commerce (DOC)

7.____

8. In federal contracts, service contract clauses are recorded on

    A. DD Form 350   B. GSA Form 3504
    C. GSA Form 3507   D. SF26

8.____

2 (#2)

9. In general, the reason a party enters into a contract, which is an essential element of a valid and enforceable contract, is known as 9

    A. validation   B. consideration
    C. capacity   D. acceptance

10. Under certain conditions (sole-source situations, unusual and compelling urgency, buying for foreign governments, etc.), government contracting by other than competitive procedures is authorized. These procurements are generally initiated by a(n) 10

    A. Invitation for Bids (IFB)
    B. Request for Quotations (RFQ)
    C. Certificate of Competency (CoC)
    D. Request for Proposals (RFP)

11. In seeking administrative or judicial remedies to a contract appeal, most appeals must be filed with the appropriate agency within _____ days of the ruling or incident. 11

    A. 10   B. 30   C. 90   D. 180

12. Under a 1963 court ruling, parties to a contract are deemed to have agreed to any contract provision required by law to be included in the contract, even if it was omitted from the written document. This is known as the _____ doctrine. 12

    A. Christian   B. quantum meruit
    C. contra proferentum   D. adhesion

13. Which of the following types of contracts is typically used when uncertainties in contract performance do not permit costs to be estimated with sufficient accuracy? 13

    A. Cost-reimbursement   B. Indefinite-quantity
    C. Time-and-materials   D. Requirements

14. For a fixed-price plus economic price adjustment contract, adjustments generally include each of the following EXCEPT those based on 14

    A. actual costs of labor or material
    B. key economic indicators
    C. cost indexes of labor or material
    D. established prices

15. Which of the following would be LEAST likely to be considered a *cardinal change* to a contract? 15

    A. Requiring a contractor to change the floor covering for an area of a hospital that is more than 12,000 square feet, forcing the contractor to turn to a different vendor for materials and hire new installment personnel
    B. Requiring a contractor to rebuild a structure after the structure initially built by the contractor collapsed due to a defective specification -- a major reconstruction that nearly doubled the contract price
    C. Ordering a contractor who is building a bag filter particle collection system, which extracts pollutants from an airstream, to withstand an internal operating pressure of 1.8 psi, when no such requirement existed in the original contract
    D. In a levee construction contract, increasing the embankment from 8,000 cubic yards to 14,000 cubic yards of earth, a change that necessitates the transport of equipment more than 100 miles back to the jobsite

3 (#2)

16. What is the term for the requirement that certain clauses in a prime contract be imposed by a prime contractor on its subcontractors?

   A. Transfer
   C. Flow-down
   B. Conveyance
   D. Assignment

16._____

17. The Federal Acquisitions Regulation's (FAR) rules for record retention require that a contractor maintain requisition records for a period of at LEAST _____ year(s).

   A. one   B. two   C. four   D. five

17._____

18. When a performance bond is used, the amount is usually _____% of the amount of the contract, and may be reduced proportionately as performance moves forward successfully.

   A. 5-10   B. 25-33   C. 50-75   D. 100

18._____

19. In the federal acquisitions process, which of the following is typically performed FIRST?

   A. Technical evaluation
   B. Negotiations
   C. Contract administration
   D. Price/cost analysis

19._____

20. For most contract appeals involving claims of $10,000 or less, the agency to whom the contractor should direct the appeal is the

   A. United States Claims Court
   B. General Services Administration Board of Appeals
   C. United States Court of Appeals for the Federal Court
   D. General Accounting Office

20._____

21. The government issues a cure *notice* to a contractor which specifies a failure to perform. Under normal conditions, how many days does the contractor have to cure the failure?

   A. 3   B. 5   C. 10   D. 30

21._____

22. Which of the following means of contract termination will result in a *black mark* on a contractor's performance record?

   I. Partial termination
   II. No-cost termination
   III. Default
   IV. Termination for convenience

The CORRECT answer is:

   A. II *only*   B. III *only*   C. III, IV   D. I, IV

22._____

23. The agreement of one party in a contract to secure the other against loss or damage which may occur in the future in connection with the performance of the contract is a(n)

   A. mutual agreement
   C. subrogation clause
   B. indemnification clause
   D. executory clause

23._____

4 (#2)

24. In government contracting, a cost-plus-fixed-fee contract is most likely to be used in _____ contracts.

    A. durable goods
    B. multiple award schedule
    C. transportation and bailment
    D. research and engineering

25. From a contractor's perspective, the biggest drawback to two-step formal advertising and bidding is

    A. rigid specifications
    B. limited opportunity to explain bid details
    C. older, outdated processes
    D. bid costs

KEY (CORRECT ANSWERS)

1.	A		11.	C
2.	C		12.	A
3.	A		13.	A
4.	C		14.	B
5.	B		15.	A
6.	B		16.	C
7.	B		17.	B
8.	B		18.	D
9.	B		19.	A
10.	B		20.	A

21.	C
22.	B
23.	B
24.	D
25.	D

EXAMINATION SECTION
TEST 1

DIRECTIONS: Each question or incomplete statement is followed by several suggested answers or completions. Select the one that BEST answers the question or completes the statement. *PRINT THE LETTER OF THE CORRECT ANSWER IN THE SPACE AT THE RIGHT.*

1. Of the following ways in which a prospective bidder may obtain a copy of an IFB, which of the following is LEAST recommended?

    A. Being selected from the bidders list
    B. Consulting the FACNET
    C. Consulting the COMMERCE BUSINESS DAILY
    D. Seeing an IFB on a bid board

1.____

2. In a contractual agreement, the duty imposed on an injured party to exercise reasonable diligence in attempting to minimize the damages resulting from the injury is known as the

    A. liquidation of damages   B. mitigation of damages
    C. force majeure   D. quid pro quo

2.____

3. A cost is considered allocable under each of the following conditions EXCEPT when it

    A. benefits both a contract and other work
    B. can be assigned in proportion to the value received by both the contract and other work
    C. is incurred for a specific contract
    D. is not determined necessary for the business but a direct link to the contract can be shown

3.____

4. When progress payments are used to finance a contract, the customary progress payment rate is _____%.

    A. 60-65   B. 70-75   C. 80-85   D. 90-95

4.____

5. The point-of-contact identified on the face of an Invitation to Bid is usually the

    A. procurement contracting officer (PCO)
    B. contract specialist
    C. administrative contracting officer (ACO)
    D. requirements person

5.____

6. Progress payments are typically made on the basis of each of the following EXCEPT

    A. performance measured by quantifiable methods
    B. a percentage of stage of completion
    C. fixed time intervals
    D. costs incurred by the contractor as work progresses

6.____

7. A government agency is evaluating a proposal which includes a technical proposal. In its evaluation, the ratio of weight given to technical considerations to that given to cost considerations will be

    A. 1:7   B. 1:3   C. 2:1   D. 3:1

7.____

2 (#1)

8. The government may sometimes establish a contract in which all of its actual purchase needs during a specified period are met by the contract, with deliveries to be scheduled by placing orders with the contractor. This is known as a(n) _____ contract.   8.__

    A. cost-reimbursement   B. requirements
    C. fixed-price   D. indefinite-quantity

9. A federal contractor is required to report any contingent fees to the contracting agency on form   9.__

    A. GSA 1171   B. OMBSFLL
    C. SF25-A   D. SF119

10. A bidder overlooks one in a series of amendments that have been made to an initial Invitation for Bids (IFB).   10.__
If the bid is otherwise responsive, the contracting officer may
    I. contact the bidder to inquire about the oversight
    II. assume, since all other amendments were signed, that the bidder agrees in principle to the terms of the IFB as amended
    III. reject the bid outright
The CORRECT answer is:

    A. I *only*   B. I, III   C. III *only*   D. II, III

11. One who undertakes to pay money or perform in the event that a principal fails to do so is termed a   11.__

    A. guarantor   B. surety   C. fiduciary   D. trustee

12. Contracting officers are generally prohibited from requiring cost or pricing data when a procurement purchase is _____ or less.   12.__

    A. $10,000   B. $50,000   C. $100,000   D. $500,000

13. The federal government's system for administering government-wide regulations on the management, acquisition, and use of automated data processing, telecommunications resources, and records management are found in the Federal   13.__

    A. Supply Service Regulations (FSSR)
    B. Acquisition Regulation (FAR)
    C. Property Management Regulations (FPMR)
    D. Information Resource Management Regulations (FIRMR)

14. Each of the following is a measure used in determining whether a bid for a government contract is *responsible* EXCEPT the   14.__

    A. adequacy of the bidder's financial resources
    B. acknowledgement of all amendments
    C. ability to comply with delivery or performance schedules
    D. bidder's performance record

15. Under current regulations, contracts exceeding _____ require the contractor to implement an organized program for placing subcontract work in labor-surplus areas.   15.__

    A. $25,000   B. $50,000   C. $100,000   D. $500,000

3 (#1)

16. Which of the following elements of the government bidding process is contrary to normal commercial practices?
The

 A. submission of bid samples
 B. firm bid rule
 C. inclusion of descriptive literature
 D. inability for a bidder to use its own forms

17. The practice of bid-rigging is explicitly prohibited by the provisions of the _____ Act.

 A. Sherman Antitrust
 B. Procurement Integrity
 C. Robinson-Patman
 D. Anti-Kickback

18. Which of the following types of proposed procurements are listed in the COMMERCE BUSINESS DAILY (CBD)?
 I. Foreign government procurements
 II. Those required within 15 days
 III. Those for services from educational institutions
 IV. Those which are classified for reasons of national security
The CORRECT answer is:

 A. I *only*
 B. I, II, III
 C. II, III
 D. III, IV

19. When a change order causes an increase or decrease in the cost or the time required for performance of the contract, the contractor should assert the right to an equitable adjustment in writing within _____ days of the receipt of the change order.

 A. 3
 B. 10
 C. 30
 D. 60

20. Which of the following elements of a government contract is most likely to have a set format?

 A. Statement of work
 B. Purchase description
 C. Product description
 D. Specification

21. The most commonly used method of cost/technical trade-off evaluation by the government in selecting contractors is usually

 A. quantitative analysis
 B. narrative analysis
 C. a numerical point scoring system
 D. normalization analysis

22. A contractor who is unable to receive government contracts because of a law, executive authority, or regulatory authority (other than the FAR) is officially considered to be

 A. decertified
 B. debarred
 C. ineligible
 D. suspended

23. What is the term for a court-appointed custodian of property belonging to a person or party determined to be unable to properly manage his property?

 A. Warden
 B. Conservator
 C. Fiduciary
 D. Trustee

4 (#1)

24. Research and development contracts are most frequently of the _____ type.   24.__

    A. labor hour   B. cost-reimbursement
    C. indefinite-delivery   D. fixed-price

25. Which of the following bids would probably be considered *nonresponsive* by the govern-   25.__
ment?
A bid

    I. in which the bidder attempts to limit its liability to the government
    II. accompanied by a notice that the product offered forbid is subject to prior sale
    III. that does not give a definite price

The CORRECT answer is:

    A. I *only*   B. I, II
    C. II, III   D. I, II, III

_____

KEY (CORRECT ANSWERS)

1.	A	11.	B
2.	B	12.	D
3.	D	13.	D
4.	C	14.	B
5.	B	15.	D
6.	C	16.	B
7.	D	17.	A
8.	B	18.	A
9.	D	19.	C
10.	C	20.	D

21.	C
22.	C
23.	B
24.	B
25.	D

_____

TEST 2

DIRECTIONS: Each question or incomplete statement is followed by several suggested answers or completions. Select the one that BEST answers the question or completes the statement. *PRINT THE LETTER OF THE CORRECT ANSWER IN THE SPACE AT THE RIGHT.*

1. Individual contracts are typically exempt from federal equal-opportunity employment pro- visions if they involve less than _____ in prime and subcontract business in any12- month period.   1.____

   A. $5,000 B. $10,000 C. $25,000 D. $50,000

2. The rule in contract law that the acceptance of an offer is effective upon dispatch by the offeree, and not upon receipt by the offeror, is known as the _____ rule.   2.____

   A. mailbox B. tender
   C. leading object D. parole evidence

3. The provisions of the Davis-Bacon Act apply to each of the following EXCEPT   3.____

   A. the transport of materials and supplies to or from the work site by employees of a construction contractor or subcontractor
   B. the manufacturing or furnishing of materials or components off-site, or their subse- quent delivery to the site by commercial suppliers or material men
   C. painting and decorating
   D. altering, remodeling, or installation on a work site of items fabricated off-site

4. If progress payments are authorized by a contract, requests for them should be submit- ted by the contractor   4.____

   A. monthly
   B. quarterly
   C. annually
   D. whenever major work stages are completed

5. After receiving a number of bids, a government agency decides to conduct a preaward survey. Under the law, this survey must be completed within _____ days.   5.____

   A. 5 calendar B. 7 working
   C. 15 calendar D. 30 working

6. The doctrine of _____ states that when a contract's terms are susceptible to more than one reasonable interpretation, with one interpretation adverse to one party and another adverse to the other, the ambiguity is ordinarily interpreted against the drafter of those terms.   6.____

   A. equitable changes B. contra proferentum
   C. least ambiguity D. quantum meruit

7. What is the term commonly used to denote the fee adjustment formula used in cost-plus- incentive-fee contracts?   7.____

   A. Target B. Split
   C. Source phase D. Share ratio

2 (#2)

8. The cancellation of a contract, which returns the parties to the positions they were in
before the contract was made, is a(n)

    A. rescission   B. abrogation
    C. repudiation   D. discharge

8._

9. A United States contractor is competing with a foreign offer for a government contract.
The domestic offer includes a business that is located in a labor-surplus area.
Under the terms of the Buy American Act, how much will be added to the foreign offer?

    A. 3%   B. 6%   C. 12%   D. 18%

9._

10. A breach of contract that is committed prior to the actual time of required performance of
a contract, which occurs when one party by declaration repudiates a contractual obligation before it is due, is described as a(n)

    A. anticipatory breach   B. unilateral breach
    C. accelerated breach   D. breach in faith

10._

11. Under the Economic Price Adjustment clause in a multiple-award schedule (MAS) contract with the Federal Supply Service, there are certain conditions under which a contractor may increase its prices. Which of the following is NOT one of these conditions?

    A. The price increase must be at least 6 months after the commencement of the con-
tract.
    B. At least 30 days must elapse between increase requests.
    C. The increase must result from a reissue or modification of the contractor's com-
mercial catalog or price-list that was the basis for the contract award.
    D. The contractor may not request an increase during the last 60 days of the contract
period.

11._

12. Contracts under the federal supply schedule program are generally of the _____ type.

    A. cost-plus-fixed-fee   B. definite-delivery
    C. requirements   D. indefinite-delivery

12._

13. In the Uniform Contract Format (UCF) for federal contracts, which of the following
appears FIRST?

    A. Packaging and marking requirements
    B. Delivery or performance specifications
    C. Contract clauses
    D. Certifications

13._

14. In federal contracting, prime contractors are generally required by law to award _____%
of their subcontract opportunities to small businesses.

    A. 5   B. 10   C. 20   D. 33

14._

15. Of the following means of micro-purchasing goods or services, which is preferred by the
government?

    A. Standard Form 44
    B. The FACNET
    C. Third-party drafts
    D. A commercial purchase card, or IMPAC

15._

3 (#2)

16. A Request for Proposals (RFP) that is submitted in the simplified contract formation (SCF) may be for a _____ contract.
   I.   cost-plus-fixed-fee
   II. firm-fixed-price
   III. cost-plus-incentive
   IV. fixed-price with economic price adjustment
   The CORRECT answer is:

   A. I *only*   B. I, III   C. II, IV   D. III, IV

17. The refusal to fulfill a voidable contract is known as

   A. negation   B. repudiation
   C. disavowal   D. disaffirmance

18. Under the mandatory approach to value engineering changeproposals, a contractor keeps _____% of the savings resulting from the approval of the change proposal if the contract is a cost-reimbursement type.

   A. 15   B. 25   C. 50   D. 75

19. In a contract, a circumstance that divests contractual liability that has already attached upon the failure of the other party to comply with its terms is a

   A. condition subsequent   B. frustration of purpose
   C. condition precedent   D. consequential damage

20. Once a contract has been awarded, a government contracting officer typically sends each of the following items of information to contractors who submitted unsuccessful proposals EXCEPT the

   A. number of proposals received
   B. results of all first article tests
   C. name and address of the contractor receiving the award
   D. number of prospective contractors solicited

21. In the Uniform Contract Format (UCF), inconsistencies in either the IFB or the contract itself are resolved by giving precedence to certain sections. In this order of priority, which of the following is ranked first?

   A. Specifications
   B. Representations and other instructions
   C. Schedule (excluding specifications)
   D. Contract clauses

22. A federal contractor wants to submit a request for progress payments. Which form must be submitted to the agency?

   A. GSA3507   B. SF18   C. SF279   D. SF1443

23. A contract cost is defined as _____ if it is assignable to one or more cost objectives on the basis of benefits received.

   A. allowable   B. reasonable
   C. allocable   D. necessary

4 (#2)

24. Current limitations on small business subcontracting arrangements state that a small business will, as a condition of the contract, expend at least _____% of the cost performance on employees of the business.

    A. 10   B. 25   C. 50   D. 75

24.___

25. Which of the following statements represent(s) a significant DIFFERENCE between the processes involved in an Invitation for Bids (IFB) and a Request for Proposals (RFP)?

    I.   IFBs are listed in the COMMERCE BUSINESS DAILY.
    II.   The closing date for IFBs is 30 days after the opening date.
    III. If there is only one proposal issued in response to an RFP, and it is the only proposal received, it will be accepted.
    IV. Proposals submitted in response to RFPs are not opened in public.

The CORRECT answer is:

    A. I *only*   B. I, II   C. III, IV   D. II, IV

25.___

KEY (CORRECT ANSWERS)

1.	B		11.	A
2.	A		12.	D
3.	B		13.	A
4.	A		14.	C
5.	B		15.	D
6.	B		16.	C
7.	D		17.	D
8.	A		18.	A
9.	C		19.	A
10.	A		20.	B

21.	C
22.	D
23.	C
24.	C
25.	C

EXAMINATION SECTION
TEST 1

DIRECTIONS: Each question or incomplete statement is followed by several suggested answers or completions. Select the one that BEST answers the question or completes the statement. *PRINT THE LETTER OF THE CORRECT ANSWER IN THE SPACE AT THE RIGHT.*

1. The one of the following which has had GREATEST effect upon size of the budget of large cities in the last twenty years is
   A. change in the organization of the city resulting from new charters
   B. increase in services rendered by the city
   C. development of independent authorities
   D. increase in the city's ability to borrow money
   E. increase in the size of the city

1.____

2. The one of the following services for which cities receive the LEAST amount of direct financial assistance from state governments is
   A. education   B. welfare   C. housing
   D. roads   E. museums

2.____

3. Major problems which face most large cities, including New York, arise from the vertical sandwiching of governments in a single area and from the many independent governments that crowd the boundaries of the central city.
   Of the following methods of solving these problems, the one which has been MOST successful in the past has been to
   A. decentralize the administration of the central city
   B. create various supra-municipal authorities which tend to integrate the activities of the metropolitan area
   C. bring the metropolitan population under a single local government
   D. set up intermunicipal coordinating agencies to solve area administrative and economic problems
   E. allow each government element in the metropolitan area to work out its own solution

3.____

4. By means of the *debt limit*, the states regulate many facets of the debt of the cities.
   The one of the following factors which is NOT regulated in this manner is the
   A. purpose for which the debt is incurred
   B. amount of debt which may be incurred
   C. terms of the notes or bonds issued by the city
   D. forms of debts which may be incurred
   E. source from which the money may be borrowed

4.____

33

2 (#1)

5. The one of the following which is a characteristic of NEITHER the state nor the federal governments, but which is a characteristic of the government of cities is that the latter   5.____
    A. is not sovereign but an agent
    B. does not have the power to raise taxes
    C. cannot enter into contracts
    D. may not make treaties with foreign countries
    E. may not coin money

Questions 6-8.

DIRECTIONS: Questions 6 through 8 are to be answered on the basis of the following paragraph.

The regressive uses of discipline is ubiquitous. Administrative architects who seek the optimum balance between structure and morale must accordingly look toward the identification and isolation of disciplinary elements. The whole range of disciplinary sanctions, from the reprimand to the dismissal presents opportunities for reciprocity and accommodation of institutional interests. When rightly seized upon, these opportunities may provide the moment and the means for fruitful exercise of leadership and collaboration.

6. The one of the following ways of reworking the ideas presented in this paragraph in order to be BEST suited for presentation in an in-service training course in supervision is: 6.____
    A. When one of your men does something wrong, talk it over with him. Tell him what he should have done. This is a chance for you to show the man that you are on his side and that you would welcome him on your side.
    B. It is not necessary to reprimand or to dismiss an employee because he needs disciplining. The alert foreman will lead and collaborate with his subordinates making discipline unnecessary.
    C. A good way to lead the men you supervise is to take those opportunities which present themselves to use the whole range of disciplinary sanctions from reprimand to dismissal as a means for enforcing collaboration.
    D. Chances to punish a man in your squad should be welcomed as opportunities to show that you are a "*good guy*" who does not bear a grudge.
    E. Before you talk to a man or have him report to the office for something he has done wrong, attempt to lead him and get him to work with you. Tell him that his actions were wrong, that you expect him not to repeat the same wrong act, and that you will take a firmer stand if the act is repeated.

7. Of the following, the PRINCIPAL point made in the paragraph is that   7.____
    A. discipline is frequently used improperly
    B. it is possible to isolate the factors entering into a disciplinary situation
    C. identification of the disciplinary elements is desirable

3 (#1)

D. disciplinary situations may be used to the advantage of the organization
E. obtaining the best relationship between organizational form and spirit, depend upon the ability to label disciplinary elements

8. The MOST novel idea presented in the paragraph is that   8._____
   A. discipline is rarely necessary
   B. discipline may be a joint action of man and supervisor
   C. there are disciplinary elements which may be identified
   D. a range of disciplinary sanctions exist
   E. it is desirable to seek for balance between structure and morale

9. When, in the process of developing a classification plan, it has been decided that   9._____
   certain positions all have distinguishing characteristics sufficiently similar to justify treating them alike in the process of selecting appointees and establishing pay rates or scales, then the kind of employment represented by such positions will be called a "class."
   According to this paragraph, a group of positions is called a class if they
   A. have distinguishing characteristics
   B. represent a kind of employment
   C. can be treated in the same manner for some functions
   D. all have the same pay rates
   E. are treated in the same manner in the development of a classification plan

Questions 10-12.

DIRECTIONS: Questions 10 through 12 are to be answered on the basis of the following paragraph.

The fundamental characteristic of the type of remote control which management needs to bridge the gap between itself and actual operations is the more effective use of records and reports—more specifically, the gathering and interpretation of the facts contained in records and reports. Facts, for management purposes, are those data (narrative and quantitative) which express in simple terms the current standing of the agency's program, work and resources in relation to the plans and policies formulated by management. They are those facts or measures (1) which permit management to compare current status with past performance and with its forecasts for the immediate future, and (2) which provide management with a reliable basis for long-range forecasting.

10. According to the above statement, a characteristic of a type of management   10._____
    control
    A. is the kind of facts contained in records and reports
    B. is narrative and quantitative data
    C. is its remoteness from actual operations
    D. is the use of records
    E. which expresses in simple terms the current standing of the agency's program, provides management with a reliable basis for long-range forecasting

35

4 (#1)

11. For management purposes, facts are, according to the paragraph,   11.____
   A. forecasts which can be compared to current status
   B. data which can be used for certain control purposes
   C. a fundamental characteristic of a type of remote control
   D. the data contained in records and reports
   E. data (narrative and quantitative) which describe the plans and policies
      formulated by management

12. An inference which can be drawn from this statement is that   12.____
   A. management which has a reliable basis for long-range forecasting has at
      its disposal a type of remote control which is needed to bridge the gap
      between itself and actual operations
   B. data which do not express in simple terms the current standing of the
      agency's program, work and resources in relationship to the plans and
      policies formulated by management, may still be facts for management
      purposes
   C. data which express relationships among the agency's program, work, and
      resources are management facts
   D. the gap between management and actual operations can only be bridged
      by characteristics which are fundamentally a type of remote control
   E. management compares current status with past performance in order to
      obtain a reliable basis for long-range forecasting

Questions 13-14.

DIRECTIONS: Questions 13 and 14 are to be answered on the basis of the following
              paragraph.

People must be selected to do the tasks involved and must be placed on a payroll in jobs
fairly priced. Each of these people must be assigned those tasks which he can perform best:
the work of each must be appraised, and good and poor work singled out appropriately. Skill in
performing assigned tasks must be developed, and the total work situation must be conducive
to sustained high performance. Finally, employees must be separated from the work force
either voluntarily or involuntarily because of inefficient or unsatisfactory performance or because
of curtailment of organizational activities.

13. A personnel function which is NOT included in the above description is   13.____
   A. classification   B. training   C. placement
   D. severance   E. service rating

14. The underlying implied purpose of the policy enunciated in the above   14.____
   paragraph is
   A. to plan for the curtailment of the organizational program when it becomes
      necessary
   B. to single out appropriate skill in performing assigned tasks
   C. to develop and maintain a high level of performance by employees

5 (#1)

D. that training employees in relation to the total work situation is essential if good and poor work are to be singled out
E. that equal money for equal work results in a total work situation which insures proper appraisal

15. Changes in program must be quickly and effectively translated into organizational adjustments if the administrative machinery is to be fully adapted to current operating needs. Continuous administrative planning is indispensable to the successful and expeditious accomplishment of such organization changes. According to this statement,
    A. the absence of continuous administrative planning must result in out-moded administrative machinery
    B. continuous administrative planning is necessary for changes in program
    C. if changes in program are quickly and effectively translated into organizational adjustments, the administrative machinery is fully adapted to current operating needs
    D. continuous administrative planning results in successful and expeditious accomplishment of organization changes
    E. if administrative machinery is not fully adapted to current operating needs, then continuous administrative planning is absent

15.____

16. The first-line supervisor executes policy as elsewhere formulated. He does not make policy. He is the element of the administrative structure closest to the employee group.
From this point of view, it follows that a MAJOR function of the first-line supervisor is to
    A. suggest desirable changes in procedure to top management
    B. prepare time schedules showing when his unit will complete a piece of work so that it will dovetail with the requirements of other units
    C. humanize policy so as to respect employee needs and interests
    D. report danger points to top management in order to forestall possible bottlenecks
    E. discipline employees who continuously break departmental rules

16.____

17. During a supervisory staff meeting, the department head said to the first-line supervisors, "*The most important job you have is to get across to the employees in your units the desirability of achieving our department's aims and the importance of the jobs they are performing toward reaching our goals.*"
In general, adoption of this point of view would tend to result in an organization
    A. in which supervisors would be faced by many disciplinary problems caused by employee reaction to the program
    B. in which less supervision is required of the work of the average employee
    C. having more clearly defined avenues of communication
    D. lacking definition; supervisors would tend to forget their primary mission of getting the assigned work completed as efficiently as possible
    E. in which most employees would be capable of taking over a supervisory position when necessary

17.____

6 (#1)

18. A supervisor, in assigning a man to a job, generally followed the policy of fitting the man to the job.
This procedure is
    A. *undesirable*; the job should be fitted to the man
    B. *desirable*; primary emphasis should be on the work to be accomplished
    C. *undesirable*; the policy does not consider human values
    D. *desirable*; setting up a definite policy and following it permits careful analysis
    E. *undesirable*; it is not always possible to fit the available man to the job

18.____

19. Assume that one of the units under your jurisdiction has 40 typists. Their skill range from 15 to 80 words a minute.
The MOST feasible of the following methods to increase the typing output of this unit is to
    A. study the various typing jobs to determine the skill requirements for each type of work and assign to each typist tasks commensurate with her skill
    B. assign the slow typists to clerical work and hire new typists
    C. assign such tasks as typing straight copy to the slower typists
    D. reduce the skill requirements necessary to produce a satisfactory quantity of work
    E. simplify procedures and keep records, memoranda, and letters short and concise

19.____

20. In a division of a department, private secretaries were assigned to members of the technical staff since each required a secretary who was familiar with his particular field and who could handle various routine matters without referring to anyone. Other members of the staff depended for their dictation and typing work upon a small pool consisting of two stenographers and two typists. Because of turnover and the difficulty of recruiting new stenographers and typists, the pool had to be discontinued.
Of the following, the MOST satisfactory way to provide stenographic and typing service for the division is to
    A. organize the private secretaries into a decentralized pool under the direction of a supervisor to whom nontechnical staff members would send requests for stenographic and typing assistance
    B. organize the private secretaries into a central pool under the direction of a supervisor to whom all staff members would send requests for stenographic and typing assistance
    C. train clerks as typists and typists as stenographers
    D. relieve stenographers and typists of jobs that can be done by messengers or clerks
    E. conserve time by using such devices as indicating minor corrections on a final draft in such a way that they can be erased and by using duplicating machines to eliminate typing many copies

20.____

7 (#1)

21. Even under perfect organizational conditions, the relationships between the line   21.____
units and the units charged with budget planning and personnel management
may be precarious at times.
The one of the following which is a MAJOR reason for this is that
   A. service units assist the head of the agency in formulating and executing
      policies
   B. line units frequently find lines of communication to the agency head
      blocked by service units
   C. there is a natural antagonism between planners and doers
   D. service units tend to become line in attitude and emphasis, and to conflict
      with operating units
   E. service units tend to function apart from the operating units

22. The one of the following which is the CHIEF reason for training supervisors is   22.____
that
   A. untrained supervisors find it difficult to train their subordinates
   B. most persons do not start as supervisors and consequently are in need of
      supervisory training
   C. training permits a higher degree of decentralization of the decision-
      making process
   D. training permits a higher degree of centralization of the decision-making
      process
   E. coordinated actions on the part of many persons pre-supposes familiarity
      with the procedures to be employed

23. The problem of determining the type of organization which should exist is   23.____
inextricably interwoven with the problem of recruitment.
In general, this statement is
   A. *correct*; since organizations are man-made, they can be changed
   B. *incorrect*; the organizational form which is most desirable is independent
      of the persons involved
   C. *correct*; the problem of organization cannot be considered apart from
      employee qualifications
   D. *incorrect*; organizational problems can be separated into many parts and
      recruitment is important in only few of these
   E. *correct*; a good recruitment program will reduce the problems of
      organization

24. The conference as an administrative tool is MOST valuable for solving problems   24.____
which
   A. are simple and within a familiar frame of reference
   B. are of long standing
   C. are novel and complex
   D. are not solvable
   E. require immediate solution

8 (#1)

25. Of the following, a recognized procedure for avoiding conflicts in the delegation 25.____
of authority is to
    A. delegate authority so as to preserve control by top management
    B. provide for a workable span of control
    C. preview all assignments periodically
    D. assign all related work to the same control
    E. use the linear method of assignment

KEY (CORRECT ANSWERS)

1.	B		11.	B
2.	E		12.	A
3.	C		13.	A
4.	E		14.	C
5.	A		15.	A
6.	A		16.	C
7.	D		17.	B
8.	B		18.	B
9.	C		19.	A
10.	D		20.	A

21.	D
22.	C
23.	C
24.	C
25.	D

TEST 2

DIRECTIONS: Each question or incomplete statement is followed by several suggested answers or completions. Select the one that BEST answers the question or completes the statement. *PRINT THE LETTER OF THE CORRECT ANSWER IN THE SPACE AT THE RIGHT.*

1. A danger which exists in any organization as complex as that required for administration of a large city is that each department comes to believe that it exists for its own sake.
    The one of the following which has been attempted in some organizations as a cure for this condition is to
    A. build up the departmental esprit de corps
    B. expand the functions and jurisdictions of the various departments so that better integration is possible
    C. develop a body of specialists in the various subject matter fields which cut across departmental lines
    D. delegate authority to the lowest possible echelon
    E. systematically transfer administrative personnel from one department to another

1.____

2. At best, the organization chart is ordinarily and necessarily an idealized picture of the intent of top management, a reflection of hopes and aims rather than a photograph of the operating facts within an organization.
    The one of the following which is the BASIC reason for this is that the organization chart
    A. does not show the flow of work within the organization
    B. speaks in terms of positions rather than of live employees
    C. frequently contains unresolved internal ambiguities
    D. is a record of past organization or of proposed future organization and never a photograph of the living organization
    E. does not label the jurisdiction assigned to each component unit

2.____

3. The drag of inadequacy is always downward. The need in administration is always for the reverse; for a department head to project his thinking to the city level, for the unit chief to try to see the problems of the department.
    The inability of a city administration to recruit administrators who can satisfy this need usually results in departments characterized by
    A. disorganization   B. poor supervision
    C. circumscribed viewpoints   D. poor public relations
    E. a lack of programs

3.____

4. When, as a result of a shift in public sentiment, the elective officers of a city are changed, is it desirable for career administrators to shift ground without performing any illegal or dishonest act in order to conform to the policies of the new elective officers?
    A. *No*; the opinions and beliefs of the career officials are the result of long experience in administration and are more reliable than those of politicians.

4.____

41

2 (#2)

B. *Yes*; only in this way can citizens, political officials, and career administrators alike have confidence in the performance of their respective functions.
C. *No*; a top career official who is so spineless as to change his views or procedures as a result of public opinion is of little value to the public service.
D. *Yes*; legal or illegal, it is necessary that a city employee carry out the orders of his superior officers
E. *No*; shifting ground with every change in administration will preclude the use of a constant overall policy.

5. Participation in developing plans which will affect levels in the organization in addition to his own, will contribute to an individual's understanding of the entire system. When possible, this should be encouraged.
This policy is, in general,
   A. *desirable*; the maintenance of any organization depends upon individual understanding
   B. *undesirable*; employees should participate only in those activities which affect their own level, otherwise conflicts in authority may arise
   C. *desirable*; an employee's will to contribute to the maintenance of an organization depends to a great extent on the level which he occupies
   D. *undesirable*; employees can be trained more efficiently and economically in an organized training program than by participating in plan development
   E. *desirable*; it will enable the employee to make intelligent suggestions for adjustment of the plan in the future

5.____

6. Constant study should be made of the information contained in reports to isolate those elements of experience which are static, those which are variable and repetitive, and those which are variable and due to chance.
Knowledge of those elements of experience in his organization which are static or constant will enable the operating official to
   A. fix responsibility for their supervision at a lower level
   B. revise the procedure in order to make the elements variable
   C. arrange for follow-up and periodic adjustment
   D. bring related data together
   E. provide a frame of reference within which detailed standards for measuremeant can be installed

6.____

7. A chief staff officer, serving as one of the immediate advisors to the department head, has demonstrated a special capacity for achieving internal agreements and for sound judgment. As a result he has been used more and more as a source of counsel and assistance by the department head. Other staff officers and line officials as well have discovered that it is wise for them to check with this colleague in advance on all problematical matters handed up to the department head.
Developments such as this are
   A. *undesirable*; they disrupt the normal lines for flow of work in an organization

7.____

3 (#2)

B. *desirable*; they allow an organization to make the most of its strength wherever such strength resides
C. *undesirable*; they tend to undermine the authority of the department head and put it in the hands of a staff officer who does not have the responsibility
D. *desirable*; they tend to resolve internal ambiguities in organization
E. *undesirable*; they make for bad morale by causing *cut throat* competition

8. A common difference among executives is that some are not content unless they are out in front of everything that concerns their organization, while others prefer to run things by pulling strings, by putting others out in front and by stepping into the breach only when necessary.
Generally speaking, an advantage this latter method of operation has over the former is that it
   A. results in a higher level of morale over a sustained period of time
   B. gets results by exhortation and direct stimulus
   C. makes it necessary to calculate integrated moves
   D. makes the personality of the executive felt further down the line
   E. results in the executive getting the reputation for being a good fellow

8.____

9. Administrators frequently have to get facts by interviewing people. Although the interview is a legitimate fact-gathering technique, it has definite limitations which should not be overlooked.
The one of the following which is an important limitation is that
   A. people who are interviewed frequently answer questions with guesses rather than admit their ignorance
   B. it is a poor way to discover the general attitude and thinking of supervisors interviewed
   C. people sometimes hesitate to give information during an interview which they will submit in written form
   D. it is a poor way to discover how well employees understand departmental policies
   E. the material obtained from the interview can usually be obtained at lower cost from existing records

9.____

10. It is desirable and advantageous to leave a maximum measure of planning responsibility to operating agencies or units, rather than to remove the responsibility to a central planning staff agency.
Adoption of the former policy (decentralized planning) would lead to
   A. *less effective* planning; operating personnel do not have the time to make long-term plans
   B. *more effective* planning; operating units are usually better equipped technically than any staff agency and consequently are in a better position to set up valid plans
   C. *less effective* planning; a central planning agency has a more objective point of view than any operating agency can achieve
   D. *more effective* planning; plans are conceived in terms of the existing situation and their execution is carried out with the will to succeed

10.____

4 (2)

E. *less effective* planning; there is little or no opportunity to check deviation from plans in the proposed set-up

Questions 11-15.

DIRECTIONS: The following sections appeared in a report on the work production of two bureaus of a department. Questions 10 through 12 are to be answered on the basis of the following information. Throughout the report, assume that each month has 4 weeks.

Each of the two bureaus maintains a chronological file. In Bureau A, every 9 months on the average, this material fills a standard legal size file cabinet sufficient for 12,000 work units. In Bureau B, the same type of cabinet is filled in 18 months. Each bureau maintains three complete years of information plus a current file. When the current file cabinet is filled, the cabinet containing the oldest material is emptied, the contents disposed of and the cabinet used for current material. The similarity of these operations makes it possible to consolidate these files with little effort.

Study of the practice of using typists as filing clerks for periods when there is no typing work showed (1) Bureau A has for the past 6 months completed a total of 1,500 filing work units a week using on the average 200 man-hours of trained file clerk time and 20 man-hours of typist time, (2) Bureau B has in the same period completed a total of 2,000 filing work units a week using on the average 125 man-hours of trained file clerk time and 60 hours of typist time. This includes all work in chronological files. Assuming that all clerks work at the same speed and that all typists work at the same speed, this indicates that work other than filing should be found for typists or that they should be given some training in the filing procedures used. It should be noted that Bureau A has not been producing the 1,600 units of technical (not filing) work per 30 day period required by Schedule K, but is at present 200 units behind. The Bureau should be allowed 3 working days to get on schedule.

11. What percentage (approximate) of the total number of filing work units completed in both units consists of the work involved in the maintenance of the chronological files?
    A. 5%   B. 10%   C. 15%   D. 20%   E. 25%

11.____

12. If the two chronological files are consolidated, the number of months which should be allowed for filling a cabinet is
    A. 2   B. 4   C. 6   D. 8   E. 14

12.____

13. The MAXIMUM number of file cabinets which can be released for other uses as a result of the consolidation recommended is
    A. 0
    B. 1
    C. 2
    D. 3
    E. not determinable on the basis of the data given

13.____

44

5 (#2)

14. If all the filing work for both units is consolidated without any diminution in the amount to be done and all filing work is done by trained file clerks, the number of clerks required (35-hour work week) is
    A. 4   B. 5   C. 6   D. 7   E. 8

14.____

15. In order to comply with the recommendation with respect to Schedule K, the present work production of Bureau A must be increased by
    A. 50%
    B. 100%
    C. 150%
    D. 200%
    E. an amount which is not determinable on the basis of the data given

15.____

16. A certain training program during World War II resulted in training of thousands of supervisors in industry. The methods of this program were later successfully applied in various governmental agencies. The program was based upon the assumption that there is an irreducible minimum of three supervisory skills. The one of these skills among the following is
    A. to know how to perform the job at hand well
    B. to be able to deal personally with workers, especially face-to-face
    C. to be able to imbue workers with the will to perform the job well
    D. to know the kind of work that is done by one's unit and the policies and procedures of one's agency
    E. the "know-how" of administrative and supervisory processes

16.____

17. A comment made by an employee about a training course was, *We never have any idea how we are getting along in that course."*
The fundamental error in training methods to which this criticism points is
    A. insufficient student participation
    B. failure to develop a feeling of need or active want for the material being presented
    C. the training sessions may be too long
    D. no attempt may have been made to connect the new material with what was already known
    E. no goals have been set for the students

17.____

18. Assume that you are attending a departmental conference on efficiency ratings at which it is proposed that a man-to-man rating scale be introduced.
You should point out that, of the following, the CHIEF weakness of the man-to-man rating scale is that
    A. it involves abstract numbers rather than concrete employee characteristics
    B. judges are unable to select their own standards for comparison
    C. the standard for comparison shifts from man to man for each person rated
    D. not every person rated is given the opportunity to serve as a standard for comparison
    E. standards for comparison will vary from judge to judge

18.____

6 (#2)

19. Assume that you are conferring with a supervisor who has assigned to his subordinates efficiency ratings which you believe to be generally too low. The supervisor argues that his ratings are generally low because his subordinates are generally inferior.
Of the following, the evidence MOST relevant to the point at issue can be secured by comparing efficiency ratings assigned by this supervisor
   A. with ratings assigned by other supervisors in the same agency
   B. this year with ratings assigned by him in previous years
   C. to men recently transferred to his unit with ratings previously earned by these men
   D. with the general city average of ratings assigned by all supervisors to all employees
   E. with the relative order of merit of his employees as determined independently by promotion test marks

19.____

20. The one of the following which is NOT among the most common of the compensable factors used in wage evaluation studies is
   A. initiative and ingenuity required
   B. physical demand
   C. responsibility for the safety of others
   D. working conditions
   E. presence of avoidable hazards

20.____

21. If independent functions are separated, there is an immediate gain in conserving special skills. If we are to make optimum use of the abilities of our employees, these skills must be conserved.
Assuming the correctness of this statement, it follows that
   A. if we are not making optimum use of employee abilities, independent functions have not been separated
   B. we are making optimum use of employee abilities if we conserve special skills
   C. we are making optimum use of employee abilities if independent functions have been separated
   D. we are not making optimum use of employee abilities if we do not conserve special skills
   E. if special skills are being conserved, independent functions need not be separated

21.____

22. A reorganization of the bureau to provide for a stenographic pool instead of individual unit stenographer will result in more stenographic help being available too each unit when it is required, and consequently will result in greater productivity for each unit. An analysis of the space requirements shows that setting up a stenographic pool will require a minimum of 400 square feet of good space. In order to obtain this space, it will be necessary to reduce the space available for technical personnel, resulting in lesser productivity for each unit.
On the basis of the above discussion, it can be stated that in order to obtain greater productivity for each unit,

22.____

7 (#2)

A. a stenographic pool should be set up
B. further analysis of the space requirement should be made
C. it is not certain as to whether or not a stenographic pool should be set up
D. the space available for each technician should be increased in order to compensate for the absence of a stenographic pool
E. a stenographic pool should not be set up

23. The adoption of a single consolidated form will mean that most of the form will not be used in any one operation. This would create waste and confusion. This conclusion is based upon the unstated hypothesis that
    A. if waste and confusion are to be avoided, a single consolidated form should be used
    B. if a single consolidated form is constructed, most of it can be used in each operation
    C. if waste and confusion are to be avoided, most of the form employed should be used
    D. most of a single consolidated form is not used
    E. a single consolidated form should not be used

23._____

24. Assume that you are studying the results of mechanizing several hand operations.
    The type of data which would be MOST useful in proving that an increase in mechanization is followed by a lower cost of operation is data which show that in
    A. some cases a lower cost of operation was not preceded by an increase in mechanization
    B. no case was a higher cost of operation preceded by a decrease in mechanization
    C. some cases a lower cost of operation was preceded by a decrease in mechanization
    D. no case was a higher cost of operation preceded by an increase in mechanization
    E. some cases an increase in mechanization was followed by a decrease in cost of operation

24._____

25. The type of data which would be MOST useful in determining if an increase in the length of rest periods is followed by an increased rate of production is data which would indicate that _____ in the length of the rest period.

25._____

    A. *decrease* in the total production never follows an increase in
    B. *increase* in the total production never follows an increase
    C. *increase* in the rate of production never follows a decrease
    D. *decrease* in the total production may follow a decrease
    E. *increase* in the total production sometimes follows an increase

8 (#2)

KEY (CORRECT ANSWERS)

1.	E	11.	C
2.	B	12.	C
3.	C	13.	B
4.	B	14.	D
5.	E	15.	E
6.	A	16.	B
7.	B	17.	E
8.	A	18.	E
9.	A	19.	C
10.	D	20.	E

21.	D
22.	C
23.	C
24.	D
25.	A

TEST 3

DIRECTIONS: Each question or incomplete statement is followed by several suggested answers or completions. Select the one that BEST answers the question or completes the statement. *PRINT THE LETTER OF THE CORRECT ANSWER IN THE SPACE AT THE RIGHT.*

1. You have been asked to answer a request from a citizen of the city. After giving the request careful consideration, you find that it cannot be granted. In answering the letter, you should begin by
   A. saying that the request cannot be granted
   B. discussing in detail the consideration you have to the request
   C. quoting the laws relating to the request
   D. explaining in detail why the request cannot be granted
   E. indicating an alternative method of achieving the end desired

1.____

2. Reports submitted to the department head should be complete to the last detail. A far as possible, summaries should be avoided.
   This statement is, in general,
   A. *correct*; only on the basis of complete information can a proper decision be reached
   B. *incorrect*; if all reports submitted were of this character, a department head would never complete his work
   C. *correct*; the decision as to what is important and what is not can only be made by the person who is responsible for the action
   D. *incorrect*; preliminary reports, obviously, cannot be complete to the last detail
   E. *correct*; summaries tend to conceal the actual state of affairs and to encourage generalizations which would not be made if the details were known; consequently, they should be avoided if possible

2.____

3. The supervisor of a large bureau, who was required in the course of business to answer a large number of letters from the public, completely formalized his responses, that is, the form and vocabulary of every letter he prepared were the same as far as possible.
   This method of solving the problem of how to handle correspondence is, in general
   A. *good*; it reduces the time and thought necessary for a response
   B. *bad*; the time required to develop a satisfactory standard form and vocabulary is usually not available in an active organization
   C. *good*; the use of standard forms causes similar requests to be answered in a similar way
   D. *bad*; the use of standard forms and vocabulary to the extent indicated results in letters in *officialese* hindering unambiguous explanation and clear understanding
   E. *good*; if this method were applied to an entire department, the answering of letters could be left to clerks and the administrators would be free for more constructive work

3.____

49

2 (#3)

4. Of the following systems of designating the pages in a looseleaf manual subject   4.____
to constant revision and addition, the MOST practicable one is to use _____ for
main divisions and _____ for subdivisions.
   A. decimals; integers   B. integers; letters
   C. integers; decimals   D. letters; integers
   E. integers; integers

5. A subordinate submits a proposed draft of a form which is being revised to   5.____
facilitate filling in the form on a typewriter. The draft shows that the captions for
each space will be printed below the space to be filled in.
This proposal is
   A. *undesirable*; it decreases visibility
   B. *desirable*; it makes the form easy to understand
   C. *undesirable*; it makes the form more difficult to understand
   D. *desirable*; it increases visibility
   E. *undesirable*; it is less compact than other layouts

6. The one of the following which is NOT an essential element of an integrated   6.____
reporting system for work-measurement is a
   A. uniform record form for accumulating data and instructions for its
      maintenance
   B. procedure for routing reports upward through the organization and routing
      summaries downward
   C. standard report form for summarizing basic records and instructions for its
      preparation
   D. method for summarizing, analyzing and presenting data from several
      reports
   E. looseleaf revisable manual which contains all procedural materials that
      are reasonably permanent and have a substantial reference value

7. Forms control only accomplishes the elimination, consolidation, and   7.____
simplification of forms. It contributes little to the elimination, consolidation, and
simplification of procedures.
This statement is
   A. *correct*; the form is static while the procedure is dynamic; consequently,
      control of one does not necessarily result in control of the other
   B. *incorrect*; forms frequently dictate the way work is laid out; consequently,
      control of one frequently results in control of the other
   C. *correct*; the procedure is primary and the form secondary; consequently,
      control of procedure will also control form
   D. *incorrect*; the form and procedure are identical from the viewpoint of work
      control; consequently, control of one means control of the other
   E. *correct*; the assurance that forms are produced and distributed
      economically has little relationship to the consolidation and simplification
      of procedures

50

3 (#3)

8. Governmental agencies frequently attempt to avoid special interest group   8.____
pressures by referring them to the predetermined legislative policy, or to the
necessity for rules and regulations applying generally to all groups and
situations.
Of the following, the MOST important weakness of this formally correct position
is that
   A. it is not tenable in the face of determined opposition
   B. it tends to legalize and formalize the informal relationships between
      citizen groups and the government
   C. the achievement of an agency's aims is in large measure dependent upon
      its ability to secure the cooperation and support of special interest groups
   D. independent groups which participate in the formulation of policy in their
      sphere of interest tend to criticize openly and to press for changes in the
      direction of their policy
   E. agencies following this policy find it difficult to decentralize their public
      relation activities as subdivisions can only refer to the agency's overall
      policy

9. One of the primary purposes of the performance budget is to improve the ability   9.____
to examine budgetary requirement by groups who have not been engaged in
the construction of the budget.
This is accomplished by
   A. making line by line appropriations
   B. making lump sum appropriations by department
   C. enumerating authorization for all expenditures
   D. standardizing the language used and the kinds of authorizations
      permitted
   E. permitting examination on the level of accomplishment

10. When engaged in budget construction or budget analysis, there is no point in   10.____
trying to determine the total or average benefits to be obtained from total
expenditures for a particular commodity or function.
The validity of this argument is USUALLY based upon the
   A. viewpoint that it is not possible to construct a functional budget
   B. theory (or phenomenon) of diminishing utility
   C. hypothesis that as governmental budgets provide in theory for minimum
      requirements, there is no need to determine total benefits
   D. assumption that such determinations are not possible
   E. false hypothesis that a comparison between expected and achieved
      results does not aid in budget construction

Questions 11-12.

DIRECTIONS: Questions 11 and 12 are to be answered on the basis of the following
              paragraph.

Production planning is mainly a process of synthesis. As a basis for the positive act of
bringing complex production elements properly together, however, analysis is necessary,
especially if improvement is to be made in an existing organization. The necessary analysis

4 (#3)

requires customary means of orientation and preliminary fact gathering with emphasis, however, on the recognition of administrative goals and of the relationship among work steps.

11. The entire process described is PRIMARILY one of 11.____
    A. taking apart, examining, and recombining
    B. deciding what changes are necessary, making the changes and checking on their value
    C. fact finding so as to provide the necessary orientation
    D. discovering just where the emphasis in production should be placed and then modifying the existing procedure so that it is placed properly
    E. recognizing administrative goals and the relationship among work steps

12. In production planning according to the above paragraph, analysis is used PRIMARILY as 12.____
    A. a means of making important changes in an organization
    B. the customary means of orientation and preliminary fact finding
    C. a development of the relationship among work steps
    D. a means for holding the entire process intact by providing a logical basis
    E. a method to obtain the facts upon which a theory can be built

Questions 13-15.

DIRECTIONS: Questions 13 through 15 are to be answered on the basis of the following paragraph.

Public administration is policy-making. But it is not autonomous, exclusive or isolated policy-making. It is policy-making on a field where mighty forces contend, forces engendered in and by society. It is policy-making subject to still other and various policy makers. Public administration is one of a number of basic political processes by which these people achieves and controls government.

13. From the point of view expressed in the above paragraph, public administration is 13.____
    A. becoming a technical field with completely objective processes
    B. the primary force in modern society
    C. a technical field which should be divorced from the actual decision-making function
    D. basically anti-democratic
    E. intimately related to politics

14. According to the above paragraph, public administration is NOT entirely 14.____
    A. a force generated in and by society
    B. subject at times to controlling influences
    C. a social process
    D. policy-making relating to administrative practices
    E. related to policy-making at lower levels

5 (#3)

15. The above paragraph asserts that public administration 15.____
    A. develops the basic and controlling policies
    B. is the result of policies made by many different forces
    C. should attempt to break through its isolated policy-making and engage on a broader field
    D. is a means of directing government
    E. is subject to the political processes by which acts are controlled

Questions 16-18.

DIRECTIONS: Questions 16 through 18 are to be answered on the basis of the following chart.

In order to understand completely the source of an employee's insecurity on his job, it is necessary to understand how he came to be, who he is and what kind of person he is away from his job. This would necessitate an understanding of those personal assets and liabilities which the employee brings to the job situation. These arise from his individual characteristics and his past experiences and established patterns of interpersonal relations. This whole area is of tremendous scope, encompassing everything included within the study of psychiatry and interpersonal relations. Therefore, it has been impracticable to consider it in detail. Attention has been focused on the relatively circumscribed area of the actual occupational situation. The factors considered those which the employee brings to the job situation and which arise from his individual characteristics and his past experience and established patterns of interpersonal relations are: intellectual-level or capacity, specific aptitudes, education, work experience, health, social and economic background, patterns of interpersonal relations and resultant personality characteristics.

16. According to the above paragraph, the one of the following fields of study which would be of LEAST importance in the study of the problem is the 16.____
    A. relationships existing among employees
    B. causes of employee insecurity in the job situation
    C. conflict, if it exists, between intellectual level and work experience
    D. distribution of intellectual achievement
    E. relationship between employee characteristics and the established pattern of interpersonal relations in the work situation

17. According to the above paragraph, in order to make a thoroughgoing and comprehensive study of the sources of employee insecurity, the field of study should include 17.____
    A. only such circumscribed areas as are involved in extra-occupational situations
    B. a study of the dominant mores of the period
    C. all branches of the science of psychology
    D. a determination of the characteristics, such as intellectual capacity, which an employee should bring to the job situation
    E. employee personality characteristics arising from previous relationships with other people

18. It is implied by this paragraph that it would be of GREATEST advantage to bring 18.____
to this problem a comprehensive knowledge of
   A. all established patterns of interpersonal relations
   B. the milieu in which the employee group is located
   C. what assets and liabilities are presented in the job situation
   D. methods of focusing attention on relatively circumscribed regions
   E. the sources of an employee's insecurity on his job

Questions 19-20.

DIRECTIONS: Questions 19 and 20 are to be answered on the basis of the following paragraph.

If, during a study, some hundreds of values of a variable (such as annual number of latenesses for each employee in a department) have been noted merely in the arbitrary order in which they happen to occur, the mind cannot properly grasp the significance of the record, the observations must be ranked or classified in some way before the characteristics of the series can be comprehended, and those comparisons, on which arguments as to causation depend, can be made with other series. A dichotomous classification is too crude; if the values are merely classified according to whether they exceed or fall short of some fixed value, a large part of the information given by the original record is lost. Numerical measurements lend themselves with peculiar readiness to a manifold classification.

19. According to the above paragraph, if the values of a variable which are gathered 19.____
during a study are classified in a few subdivisions, the MOST likely result will be
   A. an inability to grasp the signification of the record
   B. an inability to relate the series with other series
   C. a loss of much of the information in the original data
   D. a loss of the readiness with which numerical measurements lend themselves to a manifold classification
   E. that the order in which they happen to occur will be arbitrary

20. The above paragraph advocates, with respect to numerical data, the use of 20.____
   A. arbitrary order   B. comparisons with other series
   C. a two-value classification D. a many value classification
   E. all values of a variable

Questions 21-25.

DIRECTIONS: Questions 21 through 25 are to be answered on the basis of the following chart.

7 (#3)

21. The one of the following years for which average employee production was   21.____
    LOWEST was
    A. 2012   B. 2014   C. 2016   D. 2018   E. 2020

22. The average annual employee production for the ten-year period was, in   22.____
    terms of work units, MOST NEARLY
    A. 30   B. 50   C. 70   D. 80   E. 90

23. On the basis of the chart, it can be deduced that personnel needs for the   23.____
    coming year are budgeted on the basis of
    A. workload for the current year
    B. expected workload for the coming year
    C. no set plan
    D. average workload over the five years immediately preceding the period
    E. expected workload for the five coming years

24. The chart indicates that the operation is carefully programmed and that the labor 24.____
    force has been used properly.
    This opinion is
    A. *supported* by the chart; the organization has been able to meet
        emergency situations requiring much additional work without
        commensurate increase in staff
    B. *not supported* by the chart; the irregular workload shows a complete
        absence of planning
    C. *supported* by the chart; the similar shapes of the workload and labor force
        curves show that these important factors are closely related
    D. *not supported* by the chart; poor planning with respect to labor
        requirements is obvious from the chart
    E. *supported* by the chart; the average number of units of work performed in
        any 5-year period during the 10 years shows sufficient regularity to
        indicate a definite trend

25. The chart indicates that the department may be organized in such a way as to   25.____
    require a permanent minimum staff which is too large for the type of operation
    indicated.
    This opinion is
    A. *supported* by the chart; there is indication that the operation calls for an
        irreducible minimum number of employees and application of the most
        favorable work production records shows this to be too high for normal
        operation
    B. *not supported* by the chart; the absence of any sort of regularity makes it
        impossible to express any opinion with any degree of certainty
    C. *supported* by the chart; the expected close relationship between workload
        and labor force is displaced somewhat, a phenomenon which usually
        occurs as a result of a fixed minimum requirement
    D. *not supported* by the chart; the violent movement of the labor force curve
        makes it evident that no minimum requirements are in effect

8 (#3)

E. *supported* by the chart; calculation shows that the average number of employees was 84 with an average variation of 17.8, thus indicating that the minimum number of 60 persons was too high for efficient operation

---

KEY (CORRECT ANSWERS)

1.	A		11.	A
2.	B		12.	E
3.	D		13.	E
4.	C		14.	D
5.	A		15.	D
6.	E		16.	D
7.	B		17.	E
8.	C		18.	B
9.	E		19.	C
10.	B		20.	D

21.	B
22.	B
23.	A
24.	D
25.	A

EXAMINATION SECTION
TEST 1

DIRECTIONS: Each question or incomplete statement is followed by several suggested answers or completions. Select the one that BEST answers the question or completes the statement. *PRINT THE LETTER OF THE CORRECT ANSWER IN THE SPACE AT THE RIGHT.*

1. Although some kinds of instructions are best put in written form, a supervisor can give many instructions verbally.
   In which one of the following situations would verbal instructions be MOST suitable?
   A. Furnishing an employee with the details to be checked in doing a certain job
   B. Instructing an employee on the changes necessary to update the office manual used in your unit
   C. Informing a new employee where different kinds of supplies and equipment that he might need are kept
   D. Presenting an assignment to an employee who will be held accountable for following a series of steps

1.____

2. You may be asked to evaluate the organization structure of your unit.
   Which one of the following questions would you NOT expect to take up in an evaluation of this kind?
   A. Is there an employee whose personal problems are interfering with his or her work?
   B. Is there an up-to-date job description for each position in this section?
   C. Are related operations and tasks grouped together and regularly assigned together?
   D. Are responsibilities divided as far as possible, and is this division clearly understood by all employees?

2.____

3. In order to distribute and schedule work fairly and efficiently, a supervisor may wish to make a work distribution study. A simple way of getting the information necessary for such a study is to have everyone for one week keep track of each task doe and the time spent on each.
   Which one of the following situations showing up in such study would MOST clearly call for corrective action?
   A. The newest employee takes longer to do most tasks than do experienced employees.
   B. One difficult operation takes longer to do than most other operations carried out by the section.
   C. A particular employee is very frequently assigned tasks that are not similar and have no relationship to each other.
   D. The most highly skilled employee is often assigned the most difficult jobs.

3.____

2 (#1)

4. The authority to carry out a job can be delegated to a subordinate, but the supervisor remains responsible for the work of the section as a whole.
As a supervisor, which of the following rules would be the BEST one for you to follow in view of the above statement?
   A. Avoid assigning important tasks to your subordinates, because you will be blamed if anything goes wrong
   B. Be sure each subordinate understands the specific job he has been assigned, and check at intervals to make sure assignments are done properly
   C. Assign several people to every important job so that responsibility will be spread out as much as possible
   D. Have an experienced subordinate check all work done by other employees so that there will be little chance of anything going wrong

4._____

5. The human tendency to resist change is often reflected in higher rates of turnover, absenteeism, and errors whenever an important change is made in an organization. Although psychologists do not fully understand the reasons why people resist change, they believe that the resistance stems from a threat to the individual's security, that it is a form of fear of the unknown.
In light of this statement, which one of the following approaches would probably be MOST effective in preparing employees for a change in procedure in their unit?
   A. Avoid letting employees know anything about the change until the last possible moment
   B. Sympathize with employees who resent the change and let them know you share their doubts and fears
   C. Promise the employees that if the change turns out to be a poor one, you will allow them to suggest a return to the old system
   D. Make sure that employees know the reasons for the change and are aware of the benefits that are expected from it

5._____

6. Each of the following methods of encouraging employee participation in work planning has been used effectively with different kinds and sizes of employee groups.
Which one of the following methods would be MOST suitable for a group of four technically skilled employees?
   A. Discussions between the supervisor and a representative of the group
   B. A suggestion program with semi-annual awards for outstanding suggestions
   C. A group discussion summoned whenever a major problem remains unsolved for more than a month
   D. Day-to-day exchange of information, opinions, and experience

6._____

7. Of the following, the MOST important reason why a supervisor is given the authority to tell subordinates what work they should do, how they should do it, and when it should be done is that usually
   A. most people will not work unless there is someone with authority standing over them

7._____

3 (#1)

B. work is accomplished more effectively if the supervisor plans and coordinates it
C. when division of work is left up to subordinates, there is constant arguing, and very little work is accomplished
D. subordinates are not familiar with the tasks to be performed

8. Fatigue is a factor that affects productivity in all work situations. However, a brief rest period will ordinarily serve to restore a person from fatigue. According to this statement, which one of the following techniques is MOST likely to reduce the impact of fatigue on overall productivity in a unit?
   A. Scheduling several short breaks throughout the day
   B. Allowing employees to go home early
   C. Extending the lunch period an extra half hour
   D. Rotating job assignments every few weeks

8._____

9. After giving a new task to an employee, it is a good idea for a supervisor to ask specific questions to make sure that the employee grasps the essentials of the task and sees how it can be carried out. Questions which ask the employee what he thinks or how he feels about an important aspect of the task are particularly effective.
   Which one of the following questions is NOT the type of question which would be useful in the foregoing situation?
   A. Do you feel there will be any trouble meeting the 4:30 deadline?
   B. How do you feel about the kind of work we do here?
   C. Do you think that combining those two steps will work all right?
   D. Can you think of any additional equipment you may need for this process?

9._____

10. Of the following, the LEAST important reason for having a *continuous* training program is that
    A. employees may forget procedures that they have already learned
    B. employees may develop shortcuts on the job that result in inaccurate work
    C. the job continue to change because of new procedures and equipment
    D. training is one means of measuring effectiveness and productivity on the job

10._____

11. In training a new employee, it is usually advisable to break down the job into meaningful parts and have the new employee master one part before going on to the next.
    Of the following, the BEST reason for using this technique is to
    A. let the new employee know the reason for what he is doing and thus encourage him to remain in the unit
    B. make the employee aware of the importance of the work and encourage him to work harder
    C. show the employee that the work is easy so that he will be encouraged to work faster
    D. make it more likely that the employee will experience success and will be encouraged to continue learning the job

11._____

4 (#1)

12. You may occasionally find a serious error in the work of one of your subordinates.
Of the following, the BEST time to discuss such an error with an employee usually is
    A. immediately after the error is found
    B. after about two weeks, since you will also be able to point out some good things that the employee has accomplished
    C. when you have discovered a pattern of errors on the part of this employee so that he will not be able to dispute your criticism
    D. after the error results in a complaint by your own supervisor

12.____

13. For very important announcements to the staff, a supervisor should usually use both written and oral communications. For example, when a new procedure is to be introduced, the supervisor can more easily obtain the group's acceptance by giving his subordinates a rough draft of the new procedure and calling a meeting of all his subordinates.
The LEAST important benefit of this technique is that it will better enable the supervisor to
    A. explain why the change is necessary
    B. make adjustments in the new procedure to meet valid staff objections
    C. assign someone to carry out the new procedure
    D. answer questions about the new procedure

13.____

14. Assume that, while you are interviewing an individual to obtain information, the individual pauses in the middle of an answer.
The BEST of the following actions for you to take at that time is to
    A. correct any inaccuracies in what he has said
    B. remain silent until he continues
    C. explain your position on the matter being discussed
    D. explain that time is short and that he must complete his story quickly

14.____

15. When you are interviewing someone to obtain information, the BEST of the following reasons for you to repeat certain of his exact words is to
    A. assure him that appropriate action will be taken
    B. encourage him to switch to another topic of discussion
    C. assure him that you agree with his point of view
    D. encourage him to elaborate on a point he has made

15.____

16. Generally, when writing a letter, the use of precise words and concise sentences is
    A. *good*, because less time will be required to write the letter
    B. *bad*, because it is most likely that the reader will think the letter is unimportant and will not respond favorably
    C. *good*, because it is likely that your desired meaning will be conveyed to the reader
    D. *bad*, because your letter will be too brief to provide adequate information

16.____

60

5 (#1)

17. In which of the following cases would it be MOST desirable to have two cards   17.____
for one individual in a single alphabetic file?
The individual has
   A. a hyphenated surname
   B. two middle names
   C. a first name with an unusual spelling
   D. a compound first name

18. Of the following, it is MOST appropriate to use a form letter when it is necessary   18.____
to answer many
   A. requests or inquiries from a single individual
   B. follow-up letters from individuals requesting additional information
   C. request or inquiries about a single subject
   D. complaints from individuals that they have been unable to obtain various
      types of information

19. Assume that you are asked to make up a budget for your section for the coming   19.____
year, and you are told that the most important function of the budget is its
"control function."
Of the following, "control" in this context implies MOST NEARLY that
   A. you will probably be asked to justify expenditures in any category when it
      looks as though these expenditures are departing greatly from the
      amount budgeted
   B. your section will probably not be allowed to spend more than the
      budgeted amount in any given category, although it is always permissible
      to spend less
   C. your section will be required to spend the exact amount budgeted in every
      category
   D. the budget will be filed in the Office of the Comptroller so that when a
      year is over the actual expenditures can be compared with the amounts in
      the budget

20. In writing a report, the practice of taking up the LEAST important points *first*   20.____
and the most important points *last* is a
   A. *good* technique, since the final points made in a report will make the
      greatest impression on the reader
   B. *good* technique, since the material is presented in a more logical manner
      and will lead directly to the conclusions
   C. *poor* technique, since the reader's time is wasted by having to review
      irrelevant information before finishing the report
   D. *poor* technique, since it may cause the reader to lose interest in the report
      and arrive at incorrect conclusions about the report

21. Typically, when the technique of "supervision by results" is practiced, higher   21.____
management sets down, either implicitly or explicitly, certain performance
standards or goals that the subordinate is expected to meet. So long as these
standards are met, management interferes very little.
The MOST likely result of the use of this technique is that it will

6 (#1)

A. lead to ambiguity in terms of goals
B. be successful only to the extent that close direct supervision is practiced
C. make it possible to evaluate both employee and supervisory effectiveness
D. allow for complete dependence on the subordinate's part

22. When making written evaluations and reviews of the performance of subordinates, it is usually ADVISABLE to
   A. avoid informing the employee of the evaluation if it is critical because it may create hard feelings
   B. avoid informing the employee of the evaluation whether critical or favorable because it is tension-producing
   C. to permit the employee to see the evaluation but not to discuss it with him because the supervisor cannot be certain where the discussion might lead
   D. to discuss the evaluation openly with the employee because it helps the employee understand what is expected of him

23. There are a number of well-known and respected human relations principles that successful supervisors have been using for years in building good relationships with their employees.
   Which of the following does NOT illustrate such a principle?
   A. Give clear and complete instructions
   B. Let each person know how he is getting along
   C. Keep an open-door policy
   D. Make all relationships personal ones

24. Assume that it is necessary for you to give an unpleasant assignment to one of your subordinates. You expect this employee to raise some objections to this assignment.
   The MOST appropriate of the following actions for you to take FIRST is to issue the assignment
   A. *orally*, with the further statement that you will not listen to any complaints
   B. *in writing*, to forestall any complaints by the employee
   C. *orally*, permitting the employee to express his feelings
   D. *in writing*, with a note that any comments should be submitted in writing

25. Suppose you have just announced at a staff meeting with your subordinates that a radical reorganization of work will take place next week. Your subordinates at the meeting appear to be excited, tense, and worried.
   Of the following, the BEST action for you to take at that time is to
   A. schedule private conferences with each subordinate to obtain his reaction to the meeting
   B. close the meeting and tell your subordinates to return immediately to their work assignments
   C. give your subordinates some time to ask questions and discuss your announcement
   D. insist that your subordinates do not discuss your announcement among themselves or with other members of the agency

7 (#1)

KEY (CORRECT ANSWERS)

1.	C	11.	D
2.	A	12.	A
3.	C	13.	C
4.	B	14.	B
5.	D	15.	D
6.	D	16.	C
7.	B	17.	A
8.	A	18.	C
9.	B	19.	A
10.	D	20.	D

21.	C
22.	D
23.	D
24.	C
25.	C

TEST 2

DIRECTIONS: Each question or incomplete statement is followed by several suggested answers or completions. Select the one that BEST answers the question or completes the statement. *PRINT THE LETTER OF THE CORRECT ANSWER IN THE SPACE AT THE RIGHT.*

1. Of the following, the BEST way for a supervisor to increase employees' interest in their work is to
   A. allow them to make as many decisions as possible
   B. demonstrate to them that he is as technically competent as they
   C. give each employee a difficult assignment
   D. promptly convey to them instructions from higher management

1.____

2. The one of the following which is LEAST important in maintaining a high level of productivity on the part of employees is the
   A. provision of optimum physical working conditions for employees
   B. strength of employees' aspirations for promotion
   C. anticipated satisfactions which employees hope to derive from their work
   D. employees' interest in their jobs

2.____

3. Of the following, the MAJOR advantage of group problem-solving, as compared to individual problem-solving, is that groups will more readily
   A. abide by their own decisions
   B. agree with agency management
   C. devise new policies and procedures
   D. reach conclusions sooner

3.____

4. The group problem-solving conference is a useful supervisory method for getting people to reach solutions to problems.
   Of the following, the reason that groups usually reach more realistic solutions than do individuals is that
   A. individuals, as a rule, take longer than do groups in reaching decisions and are, therefore, more likely to make an error
   B. bringing people together to let them confer impresses participants with the seriousness of problems
   C. groups are generally more concerned with the future in evaluating organizational problems
   D. the erroneous opinions of group members tend to be corrected by the other members

4.____

5. A competent supervisor should be able to distinguish between human and technical problems.
   Of the following, the MAJOR difference between such problems is that serious human problems, in comparison to ordinary technical problems
   A. are remedied more quickly
   B. involve a lesser need for diagnosis
   C. are more difficult to define
   D. become known through indications which are usually the actual problem

5.____

2 (#2)

6. Of the following, the BEST justification for a public agency establishing an alcoholism program for its employees is that   6.____
   A. alcoholism has traditionally been looked upon with a certain amused tolerance by management and thereby ignored as a serious illness
   B. employees with drinking problems have twice as many on-the-job accidents, especially during the early years of the problem
   C. excessive use of alcohol is associated with personality instability hindering informal social relationships among peers and subordinates
   D. the agency's public reputation will suffer despite an employee's drinking problem being a personal matter of little public concern

7. Assume you are a manager and you find a group of maintenance employees assigned to your project drinking and playing cards for money in an incinerator room after their regular working hours.   7.____
   The one of the following actions it would be BEST for you to take is to
   A. suspend all employees immediately if there is no question in your mind as to the validity of the charges
   B. review the personnel records of those involved with the supervisor and make a joint decision on which employees should sustain penalties of loss of annual leave or fines
   C. ask the supervisor to interview each violator and submit written reports to you and thereafter consult with the supervisor about disciplinary actions
   D. deduct three days of annual leave from each employee involved if he pleads guilty in lieu of facing more serious charges

8. Assume that as a manager you must discipline a subordinate, but all of the pertinent facts necessary for a full determination of the appropriate action to take are not yet available. However, you fear that a delay in disciplinary action may damage the morale of other employees.   8.____
   The one of the following which is MOST appropriate for you to do in this matter is to
   A. take immediate disciplinary action as if all the pertinent facts were available
   B. wait until all pertinent facts are available before reaching a decision
   C. inform the subordinate that you know he is guilty, issue a stern warning, and then let him wait for your further action
   D. reduce the severity of the discipline appropriate for the violation

9. There are two standard dismissal procedures utilized by most public agencies. The first is the "open back door" policy, in which the decision of a supervisor in discharging an employee for reasons of inefficiency cannot be cancelled by the central personnel agency. The second is the "closed back door" policy, in which the central personnel agency can order the supervisor to restore the discharged employee to his position.   9.____
   Of the following, the major DISADVANTAGE of the "closed back door" policy as opposed to the "open back door" policy is that central personnel agencies are
   A. likely to approve the dismissal of employees when there is inadequate justification

3 (#2)

B. likely to revoke dismissal actions out of sympathy for employees
C. less qualified than employing agencies to evaluate the efficiency of employees
D. easily influenced by political, religious, and racial factors

10. The one of the following for which a formal grievance-handling system is LEAST useful is in
    A. reducing the frequency of employee complaints
    B. diminishing the likelihood of arbitrary action by supervisors
    C. providing an outlet for employee frustrations
    D. bringing employee problems to the attention of higher management

10.____

11. The one of the following managers whose leadership style involves the GREATEST delegation of authority to subordinates is the one who presents to subordinates
    A. his ideas and invites questions
    B. his decision and persuades them to accept it
    C. the problem, gets their suggestions, and makes his decision
    D. a tentative decision which is subject to change

11.____

12. Which of the following is MOST likely to cause employee productivity standards to be set too high?
    A. Standards of productivity are set by first-line supervisors rather than by higher level managers.
    B. Employees' opinions about productivity standards are sought through written questionnaires.
    C. Initial studies concerning productivity are conducted by staff specialists.
    D. Ideal work conditions assumed in the productivity standards are lacking in actual operations.

12.____

13. The one of the following which states the MAIN value of an organization chart for a manager is that such charts show the
    A. lines of formal authority
    B. manner in which duties are performed by each employee
    C. flow of work among employees on the same level
    D. specific responsibilities of each position

13.____

14. Which of the following BEST names the usual role of a line unit with regard to the organization's programs?
    A. Seeking publicity   B. Developing
    C. Carrying out   D. Evaluating

14.____

15. Critics of promotion *from within* a public agency argue for hiring *from outside* the agency because they believe that promotion from within leads to
    A. resentment and consequent weakened morale on the part of those not promoted
    B. the perpetuation of outdated practices and policies
    C. a more complex hiring procedure than hiring from outside the agency
    D. problems of objectively appraising someone already in the organization

15.____

4 (#2)

16. The one of the following management functions which usually can be handled   16._____
MOST effectively by a committee is the
   A. settlement of interdepartmental disputes
   B. planning of routine work schedules
   C. dissemination of information
   D. assignment of personnel

17. Assume that you are serving on a committee which is considering proposals   17._____
in order to recommend a new maintenance policy. After eliminating a number
of proposals by unanimous consent, the committee is deadlocked on three
proposals.
The one of the following which is the BEST way for the committee to reach
agreement on a proposal they could recommend is to
   A. consider and vote on each proposal separately by secret ballot
   B. examine and discuss the three proposals until the proponents of two of
      them are persuaded they are wrong
   C. reach a synthesis which incorporates the significant features of each
      proposals
   D. discuss the three proposals until the proponents of each one concede
      those aspects of the proposals about which there is disagreement

18. A commonly used training and development method for professional staff   18._____
is the case method, which utilizes the description of a situation, real or
simulated, to provide a common base for analysis, discussion, and problem-
solving.
Of the following, the MOST appropriate time to use the case method is when
professional staff needs
   A. insight into their personality problems
   B. practice in applying management concepts to their own problems
   C. practical experience in the assignment of delegated responsibilities
   D. to know how to function in many different capacities

19. The incident process is a training and development method in which trainees   19._____
are given a very brief statement of an event or o a situation presenting a job
incident or an employee problem of special significance.
Of the following, it is MOST appropriate to use the incident process when
   A. trainees need to learn to review and analyze facts before solving a
      problem
   B. there are a large number of trainees who require the same information
   C. there are too many trainees to carry on effective discussion
   D. trainees are not aware of the effect of their behavior on others

20. The one of the following types of information about which a clerical employee   20._____
is usually LEAST concerned during the orientation process is
   A. his specific job duties   B. where he will work
   C. his organization's history   D. who his associates will be

67

5 (#2)

21. The one of the following which is the MOST important limitation on the degree to which work should be broken down into specialized tasks is the point at which
    A. there ceases to be sufficient work of a specialized nature to occupy employees
    B. training costs equal the half-yearly savings derived from further specialization
    C. supervision of employees performing specialized tasks becomes more technical than supervision of general employees
    D. it becomes more difficult to replace the specialist than to replace the generalist who performs a complex set of functions

22. When a supervisor is asked for his opinion of the suitability for promotion of a subordinate, the supervisor is actually being asked to predict the subordinate's future behavior in a new role.
    Such a prediction is MOST likely to be accurate if the
    A. higher position is similar to the subordinate's current one
    B. higher position requires intangible personal qualities
    C. new position has had little personal association with the subordinate away from the job

23. In one form of the non-directive evaluation interview, the supervisor communicates his evaluation to the employee and then listens to the employee's response without making further suggestions.
    The one of the following which is the PRINCIPAL danger of this method of evaluation is that the employee is MOST likely to
    A. develop an indifferent attitude towards the supervisor
    B. fail to discover ways of improving his performance
    C. become resistant to change in the organization's structure
    D. place the blame for his shortcomings on his co-workers

24. In establishing rules for his subordinates, a superior should be PRIMARILY concerned with
    A. creating sufficient flexibility to allow for exceptions
    B. making employees aware of the reasons for the rules and the penalties for infractions
    C. establishing the strength of his own position in relation to his subordinates
    D. having his subordinates know that such rules will be imposed in a personal manner

25. The practice of conducting staff training sessions on a periodic basis is generally considered
    A. *poor*; it takes employees away from their work assignments
    B. *poor*; all staff training should be done on an individual basis
    C. *good*; it permits the regular introduction of new methods and techniques
    D. *good*; it ensures a high employee productivity rate

6 (#2)

KEY (CORRECT ANSWERS)

1.	A		11.	C
2.	A		12.	D
3.	A		13.	A
4.	D		14.	C
5.	C		15.	B
6.	B		16.	A
7.	C		17.	C
8.	B		18.	B
9.	C		19.	A
10.	A		20.	C

21.	A
22.	A
23.	B
24.	B
25.	C

EXAMINATION SECTION
TEST 1

DIRECTIONS: Each question or incomplete statement is followed by several suggested answers or completions. Select the one that BEST answers the question or completes the statement. *PRINT THE LETTER OF THE CORRECT ANSWER IN THE SPACE AT THE RIGHT.*

1. Which one of the following generalizations is MOST likely to be INACCURATE and lead to judgmental errors in communication?　　　　1.＿＿＿
   A. A supervisor must be able to read with understanding.
   B. Misunderstanding may lead to dislike.
   C. Anyone can listen to another person and understand what he means.
   D. It is usually desirable to let a speaker talk until he is finished.

2. Assume that, as a supervisor, you have been directed to inform your subordinates about the implementation of a new procedure which will affect their work.　　　　2.＿＿＿
   While communicating this information, you should do all of the following EXCEPT
   A. obtain the approval of your subordinates regarding the new procedure
   B. explain the reason for implementing the new procedure
   C. hold a staff meeting at a time convenient to most of your subordinates
   D. encourage a productive discussion of the new procedure

3. Assume that you are in charge of a section that handles requests for information on matters received from the public. One day, you observe that a clerk under your supervision is using a method to log-in requests for information that is different from the one specified by you in the past. Upon questioning the clerk, you discover that instructions changing the old procedure were delivered orally by your supervisor on a day on which you were absent from the office.　　　　3.＿＿＿
   Of the following, the MOST appropriate action for you to take is to
   A. tell the clerk to revert to the old procedure at once
   B. ask your supervisor for information about the change
   C. call your staff together and tell them that no existing procedure is to be changed unless you direct that it be done
   D. write a memo to your supervisor suggesting that all future changes in procedure are to be in writing and that they be directed to you

4. At the first meeting with your staff after appointment as a supervisor, you find considerable indifference and some hostility among the participants.　　　　4.＿＿＿
   Of the following, the MOST appropriate way to handle this situation is to
   A. disregard the attitudes displayed and continue to make your presentation until you have completed it
   B. discontinue your presentation but continue the meeting and attempt to find out the reasons for their attitudes

71

2 (#1)

    C. warm up your audience with some good-natured statements and anecdotes and then proceed with your presentation
    D. discontinue the meeting and set up personal interviews with the staff members to try to find out the reason for their attitude

5. In order to start the training of a new employee, it has been a standard practice to have him read a manual of instructions or procedures.
This method is currently being replaced by the _____ method.
    A. audio-visual   B. conference
    C. lecture   D. programmed instruction

5._____

6. Of the following subjects, the one that can usually be successfully taught by a first-line supervisor who is training his subordinates is:
    A. theory and philosophy of management
    B. human relations
    C. responsibilities of a supervisor
    D. job skills

6._____

7. Assume that as supervisor you are training a clerk who is experiencing difficulty learning a new task.
Which of the following would be the LEAST effective approach to take when trying to solve this problem? To
    A. ask questions which will reveal the clerk's understanding of the task
    B. take a different approach in explaining the task
    C. give the clerk an opportunity to ask questions about the task
    D. make sure the clerk knows you are watching his work closely

7._____

8. One school of management and supervision involves participation by employees in the setting of group goals and in the sharing of responsibility for the operation of the unit.
If this philosophy were applied to a unit consisting of professional and clerical personnel, one should expect
    A. the professional and clerical personnel to participate with equal effectiveness in operating areas and policy areas
    B. the professional personnel to participate with greater effectiveness than the clerical personnel in policy areas
    C. the clerical personnel to participate with greater effectiveness than the professional personnel in operating areas
    D. greater participation by clerical personnel but with less responsibility for their actions

8._____

9. With regard to productivity, high morale among employees generally indicates a
    A. history of high productivity
    B. nearly absolute positive correlation with high productivity
    C. predisposition to be productive under facilitating leadership and circumstances
    D. complacency which has little effect on productivity

9._____

3 (#1)

10. Assume that you are going to organize the professionals and clerks under your supervision into work groups or team of two or three employees.
Of the following, the step which is LEAST likely to foster the successful development of each group is to
    A. allow friends to work together in the group
    B. provide special help and attention to employees with no friends in their group
    C. frequently switch employees from group to group
    D. rotate jobs within the group in order to strengthen group identification

10.____

11. Following are four statements which might be made by an employee to his supervisor during a performance evaluation interview.
Which of the statements BEST provides a basis for developing a plan to improve the employee's performance?
    A. *I understand that you are dissatisfied with my work and I will try harder in the future.*
    B. *I feel that I've been making too many careless clerical errors recently.*
    C. *I am aware that I will be subject to disciplinary action if my work does not improve within one month.*
    D. *I understand that this interview is simply a requirement of your job and not a personal attack on me.*

11.____

12. Three months ago, Mr. Smith and his supervisor, Mrs. Jones, developed a plan which was intended to correct Mr. Smith's inadequate job performance. Now, during a follow-up interview, Mr. Smith, who thought his performance had satisfactorily improved, has been informed that Mrs. Jones is still dissatisfied with his work.
Of the following, it is MOST likely that the disagreement occurred because, when formulating the plan, they did NOT
    A. set realistic goals for Mr. Smith's performance
    B. set a reasonable time limit for Mr. Smith to effect his improvement in performance
    C. provide for adequate training to improve Mr. Smith's skills
    D. establish performance standards for measuring Mr. Smith's progress

12.____

13. When a supervisor delegates authority to subordinates, there are usually many problems to overcome, such as inadequately trained subordinates and poor planning.
All of the following are means of increasing the effectiveness of delegation EXCEPT:
    A. Defining assignments in the light of results expected
    B. Maintaining open lines of communication
    C. Establishing tight controls so that subordinates will stay within the bounds of the area of delegation
    D. Providing rewards for successful assumption of authority by a subordinate

13.____

4 (#1)

14. Assume that one of your subordinates has arrived late for work several times during the current month. The last time he was late you had warned him that another unexcused lateness would result informal disciplinary action.
If the employee arrives late for work again during this month, the FIRST action you should take is to
A. give the employee a chance to explain this lateness
B. give the employee a written copy of your warning
C. tell the employee that you are recommending formal disciplinary action
D. tell the employee that you will give him only one more chance before recommending formal disciplinary action

14.____

15. In trying to decide how many subordinates a manager can control directly, one of the determinants is how much the manager can reduce the frequency and time consumed in contacts with his subordinates.
Of the following, the factor which LEAST influences the number and direction of these contacts is:
A. How well the manager delegates authority
B. The rate at which the organization is changing
C. The control techniques used by the manager
D. Whether the activity is line or staff

15.____

16. Systematic rotation of employees through lateral transfer within a government organization to provide for managerial development is
A. *good*, because systematic rotation develops specialists who learn to do many jobs well
B. *bad*, because the outsider upsets the status quo of the existing organization
C. *good*, because rotation provides challenge and organizational flexibility
D. *bad*, because it is upsetting to employees to be transferred within a service

16.____

17. Assume that you are required to provide an evaluation of the performance of your subordinates.
Of the following factors, it is MOST important that the performance evaluation include a rating of each employee's
A. initiative   B. productivity   C. intelligence   D. personality

17.____

18. When preparing performance evaluations of your subordinates, one way to help assure that you are rating each employee fairly is to
A. prepare a list of all employees and all the rating factors and rate all employees on one rating factor before going on to the next factor
B. prepare a list of all your employees and all the rating factors and rate each employee on all factors before going on to the next employee
C. discuss all the ratings you anticipate giving with another supervisor in order to obtain an unbiased opinion
D. discuss each employee with his co-workers in order to obtain peer judgment of worth before doing any rating

18.____

5 (#1)

19. A managerial plan which would include the GREATEST control is a plan which   19.____
is
    A. spontaneous and geared to each new job that is received
    B. detailed and covering an extended time period
    C. long-range and generalized, allowing for various interpretations
    D. specific and prepared daily

20. Assume that you are preparing a report which includes statistical data covering   20.____
increases in budget allocations of four agencies for the past ten years.
For you to represent the statistical data pictorially or graphically within the
report is a
    A. *poor* idea, because you should be able to make statistical data
       understandable through the use of words
    B. *good* idea, because it is easier for the reader to understand pictorial
       representation rather than quantities of words conveying statistical data
    C. *poor* idea, because using pictorial representation in a report may make
       the report too expensive to print
    D. *good* idea, because a pictorial representation makes the report appear
       more attractive than the use of many words to convey the statistical data

---

KEY (CORRECT ANSWERS)

1.	C	11.	A
2.	A	12.	B
3.	B	13.	C
4.	D	14.	A
5.	D	15.	D
6.	D	16.	C
7.	D	17.	B
8.	B	18.	A
9.	C	19.	B
10.	C	20.	B

TEST 2

DIRECTIONS: Each question or incomplete statement is followed by several suggested answers or completions. Select the one that BEST answers the question or completes the statement. *PRINT THE LETTER OF THE CORRECT ANSWER IN THE SPACE AT THE RIGHT.*

1. Research studies have shown that supervisors of groups with high production records USUALLY
   A. give detailed instructions, constantly check on progress, and insist on approval of all decisions before implementation
   B. do considerable paperwork and other work similar to that performed by subordinates
   C. think of themselves as team members on the same level as others in the work group
   D. perform tasks traditionally associated with managerial functions

   1.____

2. Mr. Smith, a bureau chief, is summoned by his agency's head in a conference to discuss Mr. Jones, an accountant who works in one of the divisions of his bureau. Mr. Jones has committed an error of such magnitude as to arouse the agency head's concern.
   After agreeing with the other conferees that a severe reprimand would be the appropriate punishment, Mr. Smith SHOULD
   A. arrange for Mr. Jones to explain the reasons for his error to the agency head
   B. send a memorandum to Mr. Jones, being careful that the language emphasizes the nature of the error rather than Mr. Jones' personal faults
   C. inform Mr. Jones' immediate supervisor of the conclusion reached at the conference, and let the supervisor take the necessary action
   D. suggest to the agency head that no additional action be taken against Mr. Jones because no further damage will be caused by the error

   2.____

3. Assume that Ms. Thomson, a unit chief, has determined that the findings of an internal audit have been seriously distorted as a result of careless errors. The audit had been performed by a group of auditors in her unit and the errors were overlooked by the associate accountant in charge of the audit. Ms. Thomson has decided to delay discussing the matter with the associate accountant and the staff who performed the audit until she verifies certain details, which may require prolonged investigation.
   Mrs. Thomson's method of handling this situation is
   A. *appropriate*; employees should not be accused of wrongdoing until all the facts have been determined
   B. *inappropriate*; the employees involved may assume that the errors were considered unimportant
   C. *appropriate*; employees are more likely to change their behavior as a result of disciplinary action taken after a *cooling off* period
   D. *inappropriate*; the employees involved may have forgotten the details and become emotionally upset when confronted with the facts

   3.____

76

2 (#2)

4. After studying the financial situation in his agency, an administrative accountant   4._____
decides to recommend centralization of certain accounting functions which are
being performed in three different bureaus of the organization
The one of the following which is MOST likely to be a DISADVANTAE if this
recommendation is implemented is that
   A. there may be less coordination of the accounting procedure because
      central direction is not so close to the day-to-day problems as the
      personnel handling them in each specialized accounting unit
   B. the higher management levels would not be able to make emergency
      decisions in as timely a manner as the more involved, lower-level
      administrators who are closer to the problem
   C. it is more difficult to focus the attention of the top management in order to
      resolve accounting problems because of the many other activities top
      management is involved in at the same time
   D. the accuracy of upward and inter-unit communication may be reduced
      because centralization may require insertion of more levels of
      administration in the chain of command

5. Of the following assumptions about the role of conflict in an organization, the   5._____
one which is the MOST accurate statement of the approach of modern
management theorists is that conflict
   A. can usually be avoided or controlled
   B. serves as a vital element in organizational change
   C. works against attainment of organizational goals
   D. provides a constructive outlet for problem employees

6. Which of the following is generally regarded as the BEST approach for a   6._____
supervisor to follow in handling grievances brought by subordinates?
   A. Avoid becoming involved personally
   B. Involve the union representative in the first stage of discussion
   C. Settle the grievance as soon as possible
   D. Arrange for arbitration by a third party

7. Assume that supervisors of similar-sized accounting units in city, state, and   7._____
federal offices were interviewed and observed at their work. It was found that
the ways they acted in and viewed their roles tended to be very similar,
regardless of who employed them.
Which of the following is the BEST explanation of this similarity
   A. A supervisor will ordinarily behave in conformance to his own self-image.
   B. Each role in an organization, including the supervisory role, calls for a
      distinct type of personality.
   C. The supervisor role reflects an exceptionally complex pattern of human
      response.
   D. The general nature of the duties and responsibilities of the supervisory
      position determines the role.

77

3 (#2)

8. Which of the following is NOT consistent with the findings of recent research about the characteristics of successful top managers?
   A. They are *inner-directed* and not overly concerned with pleasing others.
   B. They are challenged by situations filled with high risk and ambiguity.
   C. They tend to stay on the same job for long periods of time.
   D. They consider it more important to handle critical assignments successfully than to do routine work well.

8.____

9. As a supervisor, you have to give subordinates operational guidelines.
   Of the following, the BEST reason for providing them with information about the overall objectives within which their operations fit is that the subordinates will
   A. be more likely to carry out the operation according to your expectations
   B. know that there is a legitimate reason for carrying out the operation in the way you have prescribed
   C. be more likely to handle unanticipated problems that may arise without having to take up your time
   D. more likely to transmit the operating instructions correctly to their subordinates

9.____

10. A supervisor holds frequent meetings with his staff.
    Of the following, the BEST approach he can take in order to elicit productive discussions at these meetings is for him to
    A. ask questions of those who attend
    B. include several levels of supervisors at the meetings
    C. hold the meetings at a specified time each week
    D. begin each meeting with a statement that discussion is welcomed

10.____

11. Of the following, the MOST important action that a supervisor can take to increase the productivity of a subordinate is to
    A. increase his uninterrupted work time
    B. increase the number of reproducing machines available in the office
    C. provide clerical assistance whenever he requests it
    D. reduce the number of his assigned tasks

11.____

12. Assume that, as a supervisor, you find out that you often must countermand or modify your original staff memos.
    If this practice continues, which one of the following situations is MOST likely to occur? The
    A. staff will not bother to read your memos
    B. office files will become cluttered
    C. staff will delay acting on your memos
    D. memos will be treated routinely

12.____

13. In making management decisions, the committee approach is often used by managers.
    Of the following, the BEST reason for using this approach is to
    A. prevent any one individual from assuming too much authority
    B. allow the manager to bring a wider range of experience and judgment to bear on the problem

13.____

4 (#2)

    C. allow the participation of all staff members, which will make them feel more committed to the decisions reached

    D. permit the rapid transmission of information about decisions reached to the staff members concerned

14. In establishing standards for the measurement of the performance of a management project team, it is MOST important for the project manager to   14.____

    A. identify and define the objectives of the project

    B. determine the number of people who will be assigned to the project team

    C. evaluate the skills of the staff who will be assigned to the project team

    D. estimate fairly accurately the length of time required to complete each phase of the project

15. It is virtually impossible to tell an employee either that he is not good as another employee or that he does not measure up to a desirable level of performance, without having him feel threatened, rejected, and discouraged.   15.____

In accordance with the foregoing observation, a supervisor who is concerned about the performance of the less efficient members of his staff should realize that

    A. he might obtain better results by not discussing the quality and quantity of their work with them, but by relying instead on the written evaluation of their performance to motivate their improvement

    B. since he is required to discuss their performance with them, he should do so in words of encouragement and in so friendly a manner as to not destroy their morale

    C. he might discuss their work in a general way, without mentioning any of the specifics about the quality of their performance, with the expectation that they would understand the full implications of his talk

    D. he should make it a point, while telling them of their poor performance, to mention that their work is as good as that of some of the other employees in the unit

16. Some advocates of management-by-objectives procedures in public agencies have been urging that this method of operations be expanded to encompass all agencies of the government, for one or more of the following reasons, not all of which may be correct: 16.____

    I. The MBO method is likely to succeed because it embraces the practice of setting near-term goals for the subordinate manager, reviewing accomplishments at an appropriate time, and repeating this process indefinitely

    II. Provision for authority to perform the tasks assigned as goals in the MBO method is normally not needed because targets are set in quantitative or qualitative terms and specific times for accomplishment are arranged in short-term, repetitive intervals

    III. Many other appraisal-of-performance programs failed because both supervisors and subordinates resisted them, while the MBO approach is not instituted until there is an organizational commitment to it

    IV. Personal accountability is clearly established through the MBO approach because verifiable results are set up in the process of formulating the targets

5 (#2)

Which of the choices below includes ALL of the foregoing statements that are CORRECT?

A. I, III   B. II, IV   C. I, II, III, IV   D. I, III, IV

17. In preparing an organizational structure, the PRINCIPAL guideline for locating staff units is to place them 17._____
    A. all under a common supervisor
    B. as close as possible to the activities they serve
    C. as close to the chief executive as possible without over-extending his span of control
    D. at the lowest operational level

18. The relative importance of any unit in a department can be LEAST reliably judged by the 18._____
    A. amount of office space allocated to the unit
    B. number of employees in the unit
    C. rank of the individual who heads the unit
    D. rank of the individual to whom the unit head reports directly

19. Those who favor Planning-Programming-Budgeting Systems (PPBS) as a new method of governmental financial administration emphasize that PPBS 19._____
    A. applies statistical measurements which correlate highly with criteria
    B. makes possible economic systems analysis, including an explicit examination of alternatives
    C. makes available scarce government resources which can be coordinated on a government-wide basis and shared between local units of government
    D. shifts the emphasis in budgeting methods to an automated system of data processing

20. The term applied to computer processing which processes data concurrently with a given activity and provides results soon enough to influence the selection of a course of action is _____ processing. 20._____
    A. realtime   B. batch
    C. random access   D. integrated data

6 (#2)

KEY (CORRECT ANSWERS)

1.	D	11.	A
2.	C	12.	C
3.	B	13.	B
4.	D	14.	A
5.	B	15.	B
6.	C	16.	D
7.	D	17.	B
8.	C	18.	B
9.	C	19.	B
10.	A	20.	A

EXAMINATION SECTION
TEST 1

DIRECTIONS: Each question or incomplete statement is followed by several suggested answers or completions. Select the one that BEST answers the question or completes the statement. *PRINT THE LETTER OF THE CORRECT ANSWER IN THE SPACE AT THE RIGHT.*

1. Which one of the following is LEAST likely to be an area or cause of trouble in the use of staff personnel?   1._____

    A. Misunderstanding of the role the staff personnel are supposed to play as a result of vagueness of definition of their duties and authority
    B. Tendency of staff personnel almost always to be older than line personnel at comparable salary levels with whom they must deal
    C. Selection of staff personnel who fail to have simultaneously both competence in their specialities and skill in staff work
    D. The staff person fails to understand mixed staff and operating duties

2. Which of the following is generally NOT a valid statement with respect to the supervisory process?   2._____

    A. General supervision is more effective than close supervision.
    B. Employee-centered supervisors lead more effectively than do production-centered supervisors.
    C. Employee satisfaction is directly related to productivity.
    D. Low-producing supervisors use techniques that are different from high-producing supervisors.

3. Which of the following is the MOST essential element for proper evaluation of the performance of subordinate supervisors?   3._____

    A. Careful definition of each supervisor's specific job responsibilities and of his progress in meeting mutually agreed upon work goals
    B. System of rewards and penalties based on each supervisor's progress in meeting clearly defined performance standards
    C. Definition of personality traits, such as industry, initiative, dependability, and cooperativeness, required for effective job performance
    D. Breakdown of each supervisor's job into separate components and a rating of his performance on each individual task

4. The PRINCIPAL advantage of specialization for the operating efficiency of a public service agency is that specialization   4._____

    A. reduces the amount of red tape in coordinating the activities of mutually dependent departments
    B. simplifies the problem of developing adequate job controls
    C. provides employees with a clear understanding of the relationship of their activities to the overall objectives of the agency
    D. reduces destructive competition for power between departments

83

2 (#1)

5. A list of conditions which encourages good morale inside a work group would NOT include a   5.____

    A. high rate of agreement among group members on values and objectives
    B. tight control system to minimize the risk of individual error
    C. good possibility that joint action will accomplish goals
    D. past history of successful group accomplishment

6. Of the following, the MOST important factor to be considered in selecting a training strategy or program is the   6.____

    A. requirements of the job to be performed by the trainees
    B. educational level or prior training of the trainees
    C. size of the training group
    D. quality and competence of available training specialists

7. Of the following, the one which is considered to be LEAST characteristic of the higher ranks of management is   7.____

    A. that higher levels of management benefit from modern technology
    B. that success is measured by the extent to which objectives are achieved
    C. the number of subordinates that directly report to a manager
    D. the de-emphasis of individual and specialized performance

8. Assume that a manager is preparing a training syllabus to be used in training members of her staff.
Which of the following would NOT be a valid principle of the learning process to consider when preparing this training syllabus?   8.____

    A. When a person has thoroughly learned a task, it takes a lot of effort to create a little more improvement.
    B. In complicated learning situations, there is a period in which an additional period of practice produces an equal amount of improvement in learning.
    C. The less a person knows about the task, the slower the initial progress.
    D. The more a person knows about the task, the slower the initial progress.

9. Which statement BEST illustrates when collective bargaining agreements are working well?   9.____

    A. Executives strongly support subordinate managers.
    B. The management rights clause in the contract is clear and enforced.
    C. Contract provisions are competently interpreted.
    D. The provisions of the agreement are properly interpreted, communicated, and observed.

3 (#1)

10. An executive who wishes to encourage subordinates to communicate freely with him about a job-related problem should FIRST

    A. state his own position on the problem before listening to the subordinates' ideas
    B. invite subordinates to give their own opinions on the problem
    C. ask subordinates for their reactions to his own ideas about the problem
    D. guard the confidentiality of management information about the problem

10._____

11. The ability to deal constructively with intra-organizational conflict is an essential attribute of the successful manager.
The one of the following types of conflict which would be LEAST difficult to handle constructively is a situation in which there is

    A. agreement on objectives, but disagreement as to the probable results of adopting the various alternatives
    B. agreement on objectives, disagreement on alternative courses of action, and relative certainty as to the outcome of one of the alternatives
    C. disagreement on objectives and on alternative courses of action, and relative certainty as to the outcome of one of the alternatives
    D. disagreement on objectives and on alternative courses of action, but uncertainty as to the outcome of the alternatives

11._____

12. Which of the following actions does NOT belong in a properly conducted grievance handling process?

    A. Gathering relevant information on why the grievance arose
    B. Formulating a personal judgment about the fairness or unfairness of the grievance at the time the grievance is presented
    C. Establishing tentative answers to the grievance
    D. Following up to see whether the solution has eliminated the difficulty

12._____

13. Grievances are generally defined as complaints expressed over work-related matters.
Which one of the following is MOST important for managers to be aware of in connection with this definition?
The

    A. fact that the definition fails to separate the subject of the grievance from the attitude of the grievant
    B. fact that anything in the organization may be the source of the grievance
    C. need to assume that dissatisfied people have adverse effects on productivity
    D. implication that management should be concerned about expressed grievances and unconcerned about unexpressed grievances

13._____

85

4 (#1)

14. In carrying out disciplinary action, the MOST important procedure for all managers to follow is to   14.____

    A. convince all levels of management on the need for discipline from the organization's viewpoint
    B. follow up on a disciplinary action and not assume that the action has been effective
    C. convince all executives that proper discipline is a legitimate tool for their use
    D. convince all executives that they need to display confidence in the organization's rules

15. Assume that an employee under your supervision is acquitted in court of criminal charges arising out of his employment.   15.____
Of the following statements concerning disciplinary action, which is MOST NEARLY correct?

    A. Disciplinary proceedings against the employee may not be held for the same offenses on which he was tried and acquitted.
    B. In a disciplinary action, the acquittal dispenses with the requirement that the employee be advised as to his constitutional rights.
    C. Civil Rights Law Section 79 prohibits the taking of any further punitive action by an employer if the offense did not involve official corruption.
    D. It is possible for the employee to be found guilty of the same offense when tried in a departmental hearing.

16. Work rules can be an effective tool in the process of personnel management.   16.____
The BEST practical definition for work rules is that they are

    A. minimum standards of conduct or performance that apply to individuals or groups at work in an organization
    B. prescriptions that serve to specialize employee behavior
    C. predetermined decisions about disciplinary action
    D. the major determinant of an organization's climate and the morale of its workforce

Questions 17-18

DIRECTIONS: Questions 17 and 18 pertain to identification of words that are incorrectly used because they are not in keeping with the meaning of the quotation. In answering each question, the first step is to read the passage and identify the incorrectly used word, and then select the word which, when substituted, BEST serves to convey the meaning of the quotation.

5 (#1)

17. Among the Housing Manager's overall responsibilities in administering a project is the prevention of the development of conditions which might lead to termination of tenancy and eviction of a tenant. Where there appears to be doubt that a tenant is fully aware of his responsibilities and is thus jeopardizing his tenancy, the Housing Manager should acquaint him with these responsibilities. Where a situation involves behavior of a tenant or a member of his family, the Housing Manager should confirm, through discussions and referrals to social agencies, correction of the conditions before they reach a state where there is no alternative but termination proceedings.

    A. Coordinate   B. Identify
    C. Assert   D. Attempt

17._____

18. The one universal administrative complaint is that the budget is inadequate. Between adequacy and inadequacy lie all degrees of adequacy. Further, human wants are modest in relation to human resources. From these two facts we may conclude that the fundamental criterion of administrative decision must be a criterion of efficiency (the degree to which the goals have been reached relative to the available resources) rather than a criterion of adequacy (the degree to which its goals have been reached). The task of the manager is to maximize social values relative to limited resources.

    A. Improve   B. Simple
    C. Limitless   D. Optimize

18._____

Questions 19-21.

DIRECTIONS: Questions 19 through 21 are to be answered SOLELY on the basis of the following situation.

    John Foley, a top administrator, is responsible for output in his organization. Because productivity had been lagging for two periods in a row, Foley decided to establish a committee of his subordinate managers to investigate the reasons for the poor performance and to make recommendations for improvements. After two meetings, the committee came to the conclusions and made the recommendations that follow.

    Output forecasts had been handed down from the top without prior consultation with middle management and first level supervision. Lines of authority and responsibility had been unclear. The planning and control process should be decentralized.

    After receiving the committee's recommendations, Foley proceeded to take the following actions. Foley decided he would retain final authority to establish quotas but would delegate to the middle managers the responsibility for meeting quotas.

    After receiving Foley's decision, the middle managers proceeded to delegate to the first-line supervisors the authority to establish their own quotas. The middle managers eventually received and combined the first-line supervisors' quotas so that these conformed to Foley's.

6 (#1)

19. Foley's decision to delegate responsibility for meeting quotas to the middle managers is inconsistent with sound management principles because

    A. Foley should not have involved himself in the first place
    B. middle managers do not have the necessary skills
    C. quotas should be established by the chief executive
    D. responsibility should not be delegated

20. The principle of co-extensiveness of responsibility and authority bears on Foley's decision.
In this case, it implies that

    A. authority should exceed responsibility
    B. authority should be delegated to match the degree of responsibility
    C. both authority and responsibility should be retained and not delegated
    D. responsibility should be delegated, but authority should be retained

21. The middle managers' decision to delegate to the first-line supervisors the authority to establish quotas was INCORRECTLY reasoned because

    A. delegation and control must go together
    B. first-line supervisors are in no position to establish quotas
    C. one cannot delegate authority that one does not possess
    D. the meeting of quotas should not be delegated

22. If one attempts to list the advantages of the management-by-exception principle as it is used in connection with the budgeting process, several distinct advantages could be cited.
Which of the following is NOT an advantage of this principle as it applies to the budgeting process?
Management-by-exception

    A. saves time
    B. identifies critical problem areas
    C. focuses attention and concentrates effort
    D. escalates the frequency and importance of budget-related decisions

23. The MOST accurate description of a budget is that

    A. a budget is made up by an organization to plan its future activities
    B. a budget specifies in dollars and cents how much is spent in a particular time period
    C. a budget specifies how much the organization to which it relates estimates it will spend over a certain period of time
    D. all plans dealing with money are budgets

19._____

20._____

21._____

22._____

23._____

7 (#1)

24. Of the following, the one which is NOT a contribution that a budget makes to organizational programming is that a budget

    24._____

    A. enables a comparison of what actually happened with what was expected
    B. stresses the need to forecast specific goals and eliminates the need to focus on tasks needed to accomplish goals
    C. may illustrate duplication of effort between interdependent activities
    D. shows the relationship between various organizational segments

25. A line-item budget is a good control budget because

    25._____

    A. it clearly specifies how the items being purchased will be used
    B. expenditures can be shown primarily for contractual services
    C. it clearly specifies what the money is buying
    D. it clearly specifies the services to be provided

KEY (CORRECT ANSWERS)

1.	B		11.	B
2.	C		12.	B
3.	A		13.	C
4.	B		14.	B
5.	B		15.	D
6.	A		16.	A
7.	A		17.	D
8.	D		18.	C
9.	D		19.	D
10.	B		20.	B

21.	C
22.	D
23.	C
24.	B
25.	C

TEST 2

DIRECTIONS: Each question or incomplete statement is followed by several suggested answers or completions. Select the one that BEST answers the question or completes the statement. *PRINT THE LETTER OF THE CORRECT ANSWER IN THE SPACE AT THE RIGHT.*

1. The insights of Chester I. Barnard have influenced the development of management thought in significant ways. He is MOST closely identified with a position that has become known as the

    A. acceptance theory of authority
    B. principle of the manager's or executive's span of control
    C. *Theory X* and *Theory Y* dichotomy
    D. unit of command principle

1._____

2. Certain conditions should exist to insure that a subordinate will decide to accept a communication as being authoritative.
Which of the following is LEAST valid as a condition which should exist?

    A. The subordinate understands the communication.
    B. At the time of the subordinate's decision, he views the communication as consistent with the organization's purpose and his personal interest.
    C. At the time of the subordinate's decision, he views the communication as more consistent with his personal purposes than with the organization's interest.
    D. The subordinate is mentally and physically able to comply with the communication.

2._____

3. In exploring the effects that employee participation has on implementing changes in work methods, certain relationships have been established between participation and productivity.
It has MOST generally been found that highest productivity occurs in groups provided with

    A. participation in the process of change only through representatives of their group
    B. no participation in the change process
    C. full participation in the change process
    D. intermittent participation in the process of change

3._____

4. The trend LEAST likely to occur in the area of employee-management relations is that

    A. employees will exert more influence on decisions affecting their interests
    B. technological change will have a stronger impact on organizations' human resources
    C. labor will judge management according to company profits
    D. government will play a larger role in balancing the interests of the parties in labor-management affairs

4._____

2 (#2)

5. Members of an organization must satisfy several fundamental psychological needs in order to be happy and productive.
The BROADEST and MOST basic needs are

    A. achievement, recognition, and acceptance
    B. competition, recognition, and accomplishment
    C. salary increments and recognition
    D. acceptance of competition and economic award

6. Morale has been defined as the capacity of a group of people to pull together steadily for a common purpose.
Morale thus defined is MOST generally dependent on

    A. job security
    B. group and individual self-confidence
    C. organizational efficiency
    D. physical health of the individuals

7. Which is the CORRECT order of steps to follow when revising office procedure?
To

    I. develop the improved method as determined by time and motion studies and effective workplace layout
    II. find out how the task is now performed
    III. apply the new method
    IV. analyze the current method

    The CORRECT answer is:
    A. IV, II, I, III
    B. II, I, III, IV
    C. I, II, IV, III
    D. II, IV, I, III

8. In contrast to broad spans of control, narrow spans of control are MOST likely to

    A. provide opportunity for more personal contact between superior and subordinate
    B. encourage decentralization
    C. stress individual initiative
    D. foster group of team effort

9. A manager is coaching a subordinate on the nature of decision-making.
She could BEST define decision-making as

    A. choosing between alternatives
    B. making diagnoses of feasible ends
    C. making diagnoses of feasible means
    D. comparing alternatives

3 (#2)

10. Of the following, the LEAST valid purpose of an organizational policy statement is to   10._____

    A. keep personnel from performing improper actions and functions on routine matters
    B. prevent the mishandling of non-routine matters
    C. provide management personnel with a tool that precludes the need for their use of judgment
    D. provide standard decisions and approaches in handling problems of a recurrent nature

11. Current thinking on bureaucratic organizations is that   11._____

    A. bureaucracy is on the way out
    B. bureaucracy, though not perfect, is unlikely to be replaced
    C. bureaucratic organizations are most effective in dealing with constant change
    D. bureaucratic organizations are most effective when dealing with sophisticated customers or clients

12. The development of alternate plans as a major step in planning will normally result in the planner's having several possible course of action available. GENERALLY, this is   12._____

    A. *desirable* since such development helps to determine the most suitable alternative and to provide for the unexpected
    B. *desirable* since such development makes the use of planning premises and constraints unnecessary
    C. *undesirable* since the planners should formulate only one way of achieving given goals at a given time
    D. *undesirable* since such action restricts efforts to modify the planning to take advantage of opportunities

13. Assume a manager carries out his responsibilities to his staff according to what is now known about managerial leadership.
Which of the following statements would MOST accurately reflect his assumptions about proper management?   13._____

    A. Efficiency in operations results from allowing the human element to participate in a minimal way.
    B. Efficient operation results from balancing work considerations with personnel considerations.
    C. Efficient operation results from a work force committed to its self-interest.
    D. Efficient operation results from staff relationships that produce a friendly work climate.

4 (#2)

14. Assume that a manager is called upon to conduct a management audit. To do this properly, he would have to take certain steps in a specific sequence. Which step should this manager take FIRST?

14._____

    A. Managerial performance must be surveyed.
    B. A method of reporting must be established.
    C. Management auditing procedures and documentation must be developed.
    D. Criteria for the audit must be established.

15. If a manager is required to conduct a scientific investigation of an organizational problem, the FIRST step he should take is to

15._____

    A. state his assumptions about the problem
    B. carry out a search for background information
    C. choose the right approach to investigate the validity of his assumptions
    D. define and state the problem

16. A manager would be correct to assert that the principle of delegation states that decisions should be made PRIMARILY

16._____

    A. by persons in an executive capacity qualified to make them
    B. by persons in a non-executive capacity
    C. at as low an organizational level of authority as practicable
    D. by the next lower level of authority

17. Of the following, which one is NOT regarded by management authorities as a fundamental characteristic of an ideal bureaucracy?

17._____

    A. Division of labor and specialization
    B. An established hierarchy
    C. Decentralization of authority
    D. A set of operating rules and regulations

18. As the number of subordinates in a manager's span of control increases, the actual number of possible relationships

18._____

    A. increases disproportionately to the number of subordinates
    B. increases in equal number to the number of subordinates
    C. reaches a stable level
    D. will first increase, then slowly decrease

5 (#2)

19. Management experts generally believe that computer-based management information systems (MIS) have greater potential for improving the process of management than any other development in recent decades.
The one of the following which MOST accurately describes the objectives of MIS is to

    A.   provide information for decision-making on planning, initiating, and controlling the operations of the various units of the organization
    B.   establish mechanization of routine functions such as clerical records, payroll, inventory, and accounts receivable in order to promote economy and efficiency
    C.   computerize decision-making on planning, initiating, organizing, and controlling the operations of an organization
    D.   provide accurate facts and figures on the various programs of the organization to be used for purposes of planning and research

19._____

20. The one of the following which is the BEST application of the *management-by-exception* principle is that this principle

    A.   stimulates communication and aids in management of crisis situations, thus reducing the frequency of decision-making
    B.   saves time and reserves top management decisions only for crisis situations, thus reducing the frequency of decision-making
    C.   stimulates communication, saves time, and reduces the frequency of decision-making
    D.   is limited to crisis-management situations

20._____

21. Generally, each organization is dependent upon the availability of qualified personnel.
Of the following, the MOST important factor affecting the availability of qualified people to each organization is

    A.   availability of public transportation
    B.   the general rise in the educational levels of our population
    C.   the rise of sentiment against racial discrimination
    D.   pressure by organized community groups

21._____

22. A fundamental responsibility of all managers is to decide what physical facilities and equipment are needed to help attain basic goals.
Good planning for the purchase and use of equipment is seldom easy to do and is complicated most by the fact that

    A.   organizations rarely have stable sources of supply
    B.   nearly all managers tend to be better at personnel planning than at equipment planning
    C.   decisions concerning physical resources are made too often on an emergency basis rather than under carefully prepared policies
    D.   legal rulings relative to depreciation fluctuate very frequently

22._____

6 (#2)

23. In attempting to reconcile managerial objectives and an individual employee's goals, it is generally LEAST desirable for management to

    A. recognize the capacity of the individual to contribute toward realization of managerial goals
    B. encourage self-development of the employee to exceed minimum job performance
    C. consider an individual employee's work separately from other employees
    D. demonstrate that an employee advances only to the extent that he contributes directly to the accomplishment of stated goals

23._____

24. As a management tool for discovering individual training needs, a job analysis would generally be of LEAST assistance in determining

    A. the performance requirements of individual jobs
    B. actual employee performance on the job
    C. acceptable standards of performance
    D. training needs for individual jobs

24._____

25. One of the major concerns of organizational managers today is how the spread of automation will affect them and the status of their positions. Realistically speaking, one can say that the MOST likely effect of our newer forms of highly automated technology on managers will be to

    A. make most top-level positions superfluous or obsolete
    B. reduce the importance of managerial work in general
    C. replace the work of managers with the work of technicians
    D. increase the importance of and demand for top managerial personnel

25._____

KEY (CORRECT ANSWERS)

1.	A	11.	B
2.	C	12.	A
3.	C	13.	B
4.	C	14.	D
5.	A	15.	D
6.	B	16.	C
7.	D	17.	C
8.	A	18.	A
9.	A	19.	A
10.	C	20.	C

21.	B
22.	C
23.	C
24.	B
25.	D

96

EXAMINATION SECTION
TEST 1

DIRECTIONS: Each question or incomplete statement is followed by several suggested answers or completions. Select the one that BEST answers the question or completes the statement. *PRINT THE LETTER OF THE CORRECT ANSWER IN THE SPACE AT THE RIGHT.*

1. The budget which shows the money to be spent to build and equip a new hospital is known as the _____ budget.   1.____

   A. capital   B. expense   C. planned   D. program

2. A significant characteristic of the program budget is that it lends itself to review and analysis.   2.____
   Why?

   A. The budget has a built-in accounting system that makes close control possible.
   B. The budget includes measurable objectives.
   C. It is possible to review performance based on units of service.
   D. All of the above

3. The advantages of program budgeting over line item and performance budgeting is: 3.____
   I. Tight, administrative control
   II. Forces the administrator to think through his total operation
   III. Measurable objectives
   IV. Simplicity of development
   V. Closer estimates of future costs
   The CORRECT answer is:

   A. I, II
   C. II, III, V
   B. II, III, IV
   D. III, IV, V

4. Of the following considerations, the one which is LEAST important in preparing a department budget request is the   4.____

   A. amounts in previous budget requests
   B. cost of material
   C. cost of personnel
   D. goals of the agency

5. The type of budget which provides the MOST flexibility in the use of appropriate funds is the _____ budget.   5.____

   A. accrual   B. item   C. line   D. program

6. A WEAKNESS of many budgetary systems today is that they   6.____

   A. are subjectively determined by those most directly involved
   B. focus on management weakness rather than management strength
   C. only show variable costs
   D. show in detail why losses are occurring

2 (#1)

7. Standards on which budgets are developed should be based PRIMARILY on 　　　　7.__

    A. a general consensus   B. agency wishes
    C. analytical studies   D. historical performance

8. The income, cost, and expense goals making up a budget are aimed at achieving a pre- 　　8.__
determined objective but do not necessarily measure the lowest possible costs.
This is PRIMARILY so because

    A. budget committees are accounting-oriented and are not sympathetic with the
supervisor's personnel problems
    B. budget committees fail to recognize the difference between direct and indirect
costs
    C. the level of expenditures provided for in a budget by budget committees is fre-
quently an arbitrary rather than a scientifically determined amount
    D. budget committees spend considerable time evaluating data to the point that the
material gathered is not representative or current

9. You, as a unit head, have been asked to submit budget estimates of staff, equipment, 　　9.__
and supplies in terms of programs for your unit for the coming fiscal year.
In addition to their use in planning, such unit budget estimates can be BEST used to

    A. reveal excessive costs in operations
    B. justify increases in the debt limit
    C. analyze employee salary adjustments
    D. predict the success of future programs

10. Which of the following is the BEST reason for budgeting a new calculating machine for 　　10.__
an office?

    A. The clerks in the office often make mistakes in adding.
    B. The machine would save time and money.
    C. It was budgeted last year but never received.
    D. All the other offices have calculating machines.

11. As an aspect of the managerial function, a budget is described BEST as a 　　11.__

    A. set of qualitative management controls over productivity
    B. tool based on historical accounting reports
    C. type of management plan expressed in quantitative terms
    D. precise estimate of future quantitative and qualitative contingencies

12. Which one of the following is *generally* accepted as the MAJOR immediate advantage of 　　12.__
installing a system of program budgeting? It

    A. encourages managers to relate their decisions to the agency's long-range goals
    B. is a replacement for the financial or fiscal budget
    C. decreases the need for managers to make trade-offs in the decision-making pro-
cess
    D. helps to adjust budget figures to provide for unexpected developments

3 (#1)

13. Of the following, the BEST means for assuring necessary responsiveness of a budgetary program to changing conditions is by   13._____

    A. overestimating budgetary expenditures by 15% and assigning the excess to unforeseen problem areas
    B. underestimating budgetary expenditures by at least 20% and setting aside a reserve account in the same amount
    C. reviewing and revising the budget at regular intervals so that it retains its character as a current document
    D. establishing *budget by exception* policies for each division in the agency

14. According to expert thought in the area of budgeting, participation in the preparation of a government agency's budget should GENERALLY involve   14._____

    A. only top management
    B. only lower levels of management
    C. all levels of the organization
    D. only a central budget office or bureau

15. Of the following, the MOST useful guide to analysis of budget estimates for the coming fiscal year is a comparison with   15._____

    A. appropriations as amended for the current fiscal year
    B. manpower requirements for the previous two years
    C. initial appropriations for the current fiscal year
    D. budget estimates for the preceding five years,

16. Line managers often request more funds for their units than are actually required to attain their current objectives.
Which one of the following is the MOST important reason for such inflated budget requests? The   16._____

    A. expectation that budget examiners will exercise their prerogative of budget cutting
    B. line manager's interest in improving the performance of his unit is thereby indicated to top management
    C. expectation that such requests will make it easier to obtain additional funds in future years
    D. opinion that it makes sense to obtain additional funds and decide later how to use them

17. Integrating budgeting with program planning and evaluation in a city agency is GENER-ALLY considered to be   17._____

    A. *undesirable*; budgeting must focus on the fiscal year at hand, whereas planning must concern itself with developments over a period of years
    B. *desirable*; budgeting facilitates the choice-making process by evaluating the financial implications of agency programs and forcing cost comparisons among them
    C. *undesirable*; accountants and statisticians with the required budgetary skills have little familiarity with the substantive programs that the agency is conducting
    D. *desirable*; such a partnership increases the budgetary skills of planners, thus promoting more effective use of public resources

4 (#1)

18. In government budgeting, the problem of relating financial transactions to the fiscal year in which they are budgeted is BEST met by

    A. determining the cash balance by comparing how much money has been received and how much has been paid out
    B. applying net revenue to the fiscal year in which they are collected as offset by relevant expenses
    C. adopting a system whereby appropriations are entered when they are received and expenditures are entered when they are paid out
    D. entering expenditures on the books when the obligation to make the expenditure is made

18.___

19. If the agency's bookkeeping system records income when it is received and expenditures when the money is paid out, this system is USUALLY known as a _____ system.

    A. cash
    C. deferred
    B. flow-payment
    D. fiscal year income

19.___

20. An audit, as the term applies to budget execution, is MOST NEARLY a

    A. procedure based on the budget estimates
    B. control exercised by the executive on the legislature in the establishment of program priorities
    C. check on the legality of expenditures and is based on the appropriations act
    D. requirement which must be met before funds can be spent

20.___

21. In government budgeting, there is a procedure known as *allotment*.
Of the following statements which relate to allotment, select the one that is MOST generally considered to be correct. Allotment

    A. increases the practice of budget units coming back to the legislative branch for supplemental appropriations
    B. is simply an example of red tape
    C. eliminates the requirement of timing of expenditures
    D. is designed to prevent waste

21.___

22. In government budgeting, the establishment of the schedules of allotments is MOST generally the responsibility of the

    A. budget unit and the legislature
    B. budget unit and the executive
    C. budget unit only
    D. executive and the legislature

22.___

23. Of the following statements relating to preparation of an organization's budget request, which is the MOST generally valid precaution?

    A. Give specific instructions on the format of budget requests and required supporting data.
    B. Because of the complexity of preparing a budget request, avoid argumentation to support the requests
    C. Put requests in whatever format is desirable.
    D. Consider that final approval will be given to initial estimates.

23.___

5 (#1)

Question 24.

DIRECTIONS: Answer Question 24 on the basis of the following information.

Sample Budget

Environmental Safety
Air Pollution Protection

Personal Services	$20,000,000	
Contractual Services	4,000,000	
Supplies and Materials	4,000,000	
Capital Outlay	2,000,000	
Total Air Pollution Protection		$30,000,000

Water Pollution Protection

Personal Services	$23,000,000	
Supplies and Materials	4,500,000	
Capital Outlay	20,500,000	
Total Water Pollution Protection		$48,000,000
Total Environmental Safety		$78,000,000

24. Based on the above budget, which is the MOST valid statement? 24._____

    A. Environmental Safety, Air Pollution Protection, and Water Pollution Protection could all be considered program elements.
    B. The object listings included water pollution protection and capital outlay.
    C. Examples of the program element listings in the above are personal services and supplies and materials.
    D. Contractual Services and Environmental Safety were the program element listings.

25. Which of the following is NOT an advantage of a program budget over a line-item budget? 25._____
A program budget

    A. allows us to set up priority lists in deciding what activities we will spend our money on
    B. gives us more control over expenditures than a line-item budget
    C. is more informative in that we know the broad purposes of spending money
    D. enables us to see if one program is getting much less money than the others

26. Of the following statements which relate to the budget process in a well-organized government, select the one that is MOST NEARLY correct. 26._____

    A. The budget cycle is the step-by-step process which is repeated each and every fiscal year.
    B. Securing approval of the budget does not take place within the budget cycle.
    C. The development of a new budget and putting it into effect is a two-step process known as the budget cycle.
    D. The fiscal period, usually a fiscal year, has no relation to the budget cycle.

6 (#1)

27. If a manager were asked what PPBS stands for, he would be right if he said 27.

    A. public planning budgeting system
    B. planning programming budgeting system
    C. planning projections budgeting system
    D. programming procedures budgeting system

Questions 28-29

DIRECTIONS: Answer Questions 28 and 29 on the basis of the following information.

Sample Budget

	Amount
Refuse Collection	
Personal Services	$ 30,000
Contractual Services	5,000
Supplies and Materials	5,000
Capital Outlay	10,000
	$ 50,000
Residential Collections	
Dwellings—1 pickup per week	1,000
Tons of refuse collected per year	375
Cost of collections per ton	$ 8
Cost per dwelling pickup per year	$ 3
Total annual cost	$ 3,000

28. The sample budget shown is a simplified example of a _____ budget. 28

    A. factorial   B. performance
    C. qualitative   D. rational

29. The budget shown in the sample differs CHIEFLY from line-item and program budgets in 29
that it includes

    A. objects of expenditure but not activities or functions
    B. only activities, functions, and controls
    C. activities and functions, but not objects of expenditure
    D. levels of service

30. Performance budgeting focuses PRIMARY attention upon which one of the following? 30
The

    A. things to be acquired, such as supplies and equipment
    B. general character and relative importance of the work to be done or the service to
       be rendered
    C. list of personnel to be employed, by specific title
    D. separation of employee performance evaluations from employee compensation

7 (#1)

KEY (CORRECT ANSWERS)

1.	A		16.	A
2.	B		17.	B
3.	C		18.	D
4.	A		19.	A
5.	D		20.	C
6.	A		21.	D
7.	C		22.	C
8.	C		23.	A
9.	A		24.	A
10.	B		25.	B
11.	C		26.	A
12.	A		27.	B
13.	C		28.	B
14.	C		29.	D
15.	A		30.	B

TEST 2

DIRECTIONS: Each question or incomplete statement is followed by several suggested answers or completions. Select the one that BEST answers the question or completes the statement. *PRINT THE LETTER OF THE CORRECT ANSWER IN THE SPACE AT THE RIGHT.*

1. Of the following, the FIRST step in the installation and operation of a performance budgeting system generally should be the

    A. identification of program costs in relationship to the accounting system and operating structure
    B. identification of the specific end results of past programs in other jurisdictions
    C. identification of work programs that are meaningful for management purposes
    D. establishment of organizational structures each containing only one work program

1.___

2. Of the following, the MOST important purpose of a system of quarterly allotments of appropriated funds generally is to enable the

    A. head of the judicial branch to determine the legality of agency requests for budget increases
    B. operating agencies of government to upgrade the quality of their services without increasing costs
    C. head of the executive branch to control the rate at which the operating agencies obligate and expend funds
    D. operating agencies of government to avoid payment for services which have not been properly rendered by employees

2.___

3. In the preparation of the agency's budget, the agency's central budget office has two responsibilities: program review and management improvement.
Which one of the following questions concerning an operating agency's program is MOST closely related to the agency budget officer's program review responsibility?

    A. Can expenditures for supplies, materials, or equipment be reduced?
    B. Will improved work methods contribute to a more effective program?
    C. What is the relative importance of this program as compared with other programs?
    D. Will a realignment of responsibilities contribute to a higher level of program performance?

3.___

Questions 4-9.

DIRECTIONS: Questions 4 through 9 are to be answered only on the basis of the information contained in the charts below which relate to the budget allocations of City X, a small suburban community. The charts depict the annual budget allocations by Department and by Expenditures over a five-year period.

104

2 (#2)

CITY X BUDGET IN MILLIONS OF DOLLARS

TABLE I.   Budget Allocations by Department

Department	2017	2018	2019	2020	2021
Public Safety	30	45	50	40	50
Health and Welfare	50	75	90	60	70
Engineering	5	8	10	5	8
Human Resources	10	12	20	10	22
Conservation and Environment	10	15	20	20	15
Education and Development	15	25	35	15	15
TOTAL BUDGET	120	180	225	150	180

TABLE II.   Budget Allocations by Expenditures

Category	2017	2018	2019	2020	2021
Raw Materials and Machinery	36	63	68	30	98
Capital Outlay	12	27	56	15	18
Personal Services	72	90	101	105	64
TOTAL BUDGET	120	180	225	150	160

4. The year in which the SMALLEST percentage of the total annual budget was allocated to   4.____
the Department of Education and Development is

    A. 2017   B. 2018   C. 2020   D. 2021

5. Assume that in 2020 the Department of Conservation and Environment divided its   5.____
annual budget into the three categories of expenditures and in exactly the same pro-
portion as the budget shown in Table II for the year 2020. The amount allocated for capital outlay in the Department of Conservation and Environment's 2020 budget was MOST
NEARLY _____ million.

    A. $2   B. $4   C. $6   D. $10

6. From the year 2018 to the year 2020, the sum of the annual budgets for the Departments   6.____
of Public Safety and Engineering showed an overall _____ million.

    A. decline of $8   B. increase of $7
    C. decline of $15   D. increase of $22

7. The LARGEST dollar increase in departmental budget allocations from one year to the   7.____
next was in

    A. Public Safety from 2017 to 2018
    B. Health and Welfare from 2017 to 2018
    C. Education and Development from 2019 to 2020
    D. Human Resources from 2019 to 2020

8. During the five-year period, the annual budget of the Department of Human Resources   8.____
was greater than the annual budget for the Department of Conservation and Environment in _____ of the years.

    A. none   B. one   C. two   D. three

3 (#2)

9. If the total City X budget increases at the same rate from 2021 to 2022 as it did from   9._
   2020 to 2021, the total City X budget for 2022 will be MOST NEARLY _____ million.

   A. $180   B. $200   C. $210   D. $215

10. The one of the following which is LEAST important in developing a budget for the next fis-   10._
    cal year for project maintenance is the

    A. adequacy of the current year's budget
    B. changes in workload that can be anticipated
    C. budget restrictions indicated in a memorandum covering budget preparations
    D. staff reassignments which are expected during the next fiscal year

11. The performance budget used by the department places MOST emphasis on   11._

    A. building facilities   B. equipment costs
    C. personnel costs   D. services rendered

12. The LARGEST part of the expenditures of the department is for   12._

    A. equipment   B. maintenance
    C. operating materials   D. personnel services

13. The department function which requires the GREATEST expenditure of funds is   13._

    A. refuse collection   B. refuse disposal
    C. snow removal   D. street cleaning

14. A FIRST step in budget preparation is *usually*   14._

    A. a realistic attempt to satisfy all unit requests
    B. forecasting the amount of various kinds of work to be done during the coming bud-
        get year
    C. an effort to increase work output
    D. appraising the quality of work done in the previous year

15. There are various types of budgets which are used to measure different government   15._
    activities.
    The type of budget which *particularly* measures input of resource as compared with
    output of service is the _____ budget.

    A. capital   B. traditional   C. performance   D. program

16. The budget for a given cost during a given period was $100,000. The actual cost   16._
    for the period was $90,000. Based upon these facts, one should say that the
    responsible manager has done a better than expected job in controlling the
    cost if the cost is

    A. variable and actual production equaled budgeted production
    B. a discretionary fixed cost and actual production equaled budgeted production
    C. variable and actual production was 90% of budgeted production
    D. variable and actual production was 80% of budgeted production

106

4 (#2)

17. In most municipal budgeting systems involving capital and operating budgets, the leasing or renting of facilities is usually shown in 17.____

    A. the operating budget   B. the capital budget
    C. a separate schedule   D. either budget

18. New York City's budgeting procedure is unusual in that budget appropriations are considered in two parts, as follows: _____ budget and _____ budget. 18.____

    A. capital; income   B. expense; income
    C. revenue; expense   D. expense; capital

19. Budget planning is MOST useful when it achieves 19.____

    A. cost control   B. forecast of receipts
    C. performance review   D. personnel reduction

20. After a budget has been developed, it serves to 20.____

    A. assist the accounting department in posting expenditures
    B. measure the effectiveness of department managers
    C. provide a yardstick against which actual costs are measured
    D. provide the operating department with total expenditures to date

21. A budget is a plan whereby a goal is set for future operations. It affords a medium for comparing actual expenditures with planned expenditures.
The one of the following which is the MOST accurate statement on the basis of this statement is that 21.____

    A. the budget serves as an accurate measure of past as well as future expenditures
    B. the budget presents an estimate of expenditures to be made in the future
    C. budget estimates should be based upon past budget requirements
    D. planned expenditures usually fall short of actual expenditures

22. If one attempts to list the advantages of the management-by-exception principle as it is used in connection with the budgeting process, several distinct advantages could be cited.
Which of the following is NOT an advantage of this principle as it applies to the budgeting process? Management-by-exception 22.____

    A. saves time
    B. identifies critical problem areas
    C. focuses attention and concentrates effort
    D. escalates the frequency and importance of budget-related decisions

23. Of the following statements that relate to a budget, select the one that is MOST accurate. 23.____

    A. A budget is made up by an organization to plan its future activities.
    B. A budget specifies how much the organization to which it relates estimates it will spend over a certain period of time.
    C. A budget specifies in dollars and cents how much is spent in a particular time period.
    D. All plans dealing with money are budgets.

5 (#2)

24. Of the following, the one which is NOT a contribution that a budget makes to organizational programming is that a budget

    24.___

    A. enables a comparison of what actually happened with what was expected
    B. stresses the need to forecast specific goals and eliminates the need to focus on tasks needed to accomplish goals
    C. may illustrate duplication of effort between interdependent activities
    D. shows the relationship between various organizational segments

25. A line-item budget is a GOOD control budget because

    25.___

    A. it clearly specifies how the items being purchased will be used
    B. expenditures can be shown primarily for contractual services
    C. it clearly specifies what the money is buying
    D. it clearly specifies the services to be provide

KEY (CORRECT ANSWERS)

1.	C	11.	D
2.	C	12.	D
3.	C	13.	A
4.	D	14.	B
5.	A	15.	C
6.	A	16.	A
7.	B	17.	A
8.	B	18.	D
9.	D	19.	A
10.	D	20.	C

21.	B
22.	D
23.	B
24.	B
25.	C

EXAMINATION SECTION
TEST 1

DIRECTIONS: Each question or incomplete statement is followed by several suggested answers or completions. Select the one that BEST answers the question or completes the statement. *PRINT THE LETTER OF THE CORRECT ANSWER IN THE SPACE AT THE RIGHT.*

Questions 1 and 2 are to be answered in accordance with the following statement.

The process of validating a factual proposition is quite distinct from the process of validating a value judgment. The former is validated by its agreement with the facts, the latter by human authority.

1. According to the above statement, the one of the following methods which is MOST acceptable for determining whether or not a proposition is factually correct is to   1.____

   A. prove that a related proposition is factually correct
   B. derive it logically from accepted assumptions
   C. show that it will lead to desired results
   D. compare it with experience

2. Assuming that the above statement is correct, the theory that the correctness of all ethical propositions can be tested empirically is   2.____

   A. *correct,* testing empirically is validating by agreement with facts
   B. *incorrect,* ethical propositions are value judgments
   C. *correct,* ethical propositions are based on rational hypotheses
   D. *incorrect, a* factual proposition is validated by its agreement with facts

Questions 3 and 4 are to be answered on the basis of the following passage.

Ideally, then, the process of budget formulation would consist of a flow of directives down the organization, and a reverse flow of recommendations in terms of alternatives among which selection would be made at every level. Ideally, also, a change in the recommendations at any level would require reconsideration and revision at all lower levels. By a process of successive approximation, everything would be taken into account and all points of view harmonized. Such a process, however, would be ideal only if the future could be foreseen clearly and time did not matter. As it is, in a complicated organization like the Federal government, the initial policy objectives established for the budget become out-of-date, before such a procedure could be carried through. While this difficulty does not in any way impugn the principle that the budget should be considered in terms of alternatives, it may call for short-cut methods of estimation rather than long drawn-out ones.

3. According to the above passage,   3.____

   A. the ideal method for estimating purposes is a short one
   B. the ideal method is not ideal for use in the Federal government
   C. directives should flow up and down via short methods
   D. the Federal government needs to speed up its reverse flow of recommendations for greater budgetary estimates

109

2 (#1)

4. A suitable title for the above passage would be 4._

    A. FORMULATING THE FEDERAL GOVERNMENT'S BUDGETARY PRINCIPLES
    B. DIRECTIVES AND RECOMMENDATIONS: BUDGETARY FLOW
    C. THE PROCESS OF BUDGET FORMULATION
    D. THE APPLICATION OF THE IDEAL ESTIMATE TO THE FEDERAL GOVERN-
       MENT

Questions 5 and 6 are to be answered in accordance with the following passage.

For purposes of budget formulation, the association of budgeting with accounting is less fortunate. Preparing for the future and recording the past do not necessarily require the same aptitudes or attitudes. The task of the accountant is to record past transactions in meticulous detail. Budgeting involves estimates of an uncertain future. But, because of the influence of accounts, government's budgets are prepared in a degree of detail that is quite unwarranted by the uncertain assumptions on which the estimates are based. A major source of government waste could be eliminated if estimates were prepared in no greater detail than was justified by their accuracy.

5. The author of the above paragraph 5._

    A. is undermining the accounting profession
    B. believes accountants dwell solely in the past and cannot deal with the future effi-
       ciently
    C. wants the accountants out of government unless they become more accurate in
       their findings
    D. wishes to redirect the accountants' handling of budgetary procedures

6. The author's attitude appears to be 6._

    A. tongue-in-cheek   B. morose
    C. strident   D. constructive

Questions 7 through 9 are to be answered SOLELY on the basis of the following situation.

John Foley, a top administrator, is responsible for output in his organization. Because productivity had been lagging for two periods in a row, Foley decided to establish a committee of his subordinate managers to investigate the reasons for the poor performance and to make recommendations for improvements. After two meetings, the committee came to the conclusions and made the recommendations that follow.

Output forecasts had been handed down from the top without prior consultation with middle management and first level supervision. Lines of authority and responsibility had been unclear. The planning and control process should be decentralized.

After receiving the committee's recommendations, Foley proceeded to take the following actions. Foley decided he would retain final authority to establish quotas but would delegate to the middle managers the responsibility for meeting quotas.

After receiving Foley's decision, the middle managers proceeded to delegate to the first-line supervisors the authority to establish their own quotas. The middle managers eventually received and combined the first-line supervisors' quotas so that these conformed to Foley's.

110

3 (#1)

7. Foley's decision to delegate responsibility for meeting quotas to the middle managers is inconsistent with sound management principles because

   A. Foley should not have involved himself in the first place
   B. middle managers do not have the necessary skills
   C. quotas should be established by the chief executive
   D. responsibility should not be delegated

7.____

8. The principle of co-extensiveness of responsibility and authority bears on Foley's decision.
   In this case, it implies that

   A. authority should exceed responsibility
   B. authority should be delegated to match the degree of responsibility
   C. both authority and responsibility should be retained and not delegated
   D. responsibility should be delegated, but authority should be retained

8.____

9. The middle managers' decision to delegate to the first-line supervisors the authority to establish quotas was INCORRECTLY reasoned because

   A. delegation and control must go together
   B. first-line supervisors are in no position to establish quotas
   C. one cannot delegate authority that one does not possess
   D. the meeting of quotas should not be delegated

9.____

Questions 10 through 13 are to be answered SOLELY on the basis of the information contained in the following passage.

The Commissioner and, with the approval of the Commissioner, the Inspectors General and any person under the supervision of the Commissioner or Inspectors General may require any officer or employee of the city to answer questions concerning any matter related to the performance of his or her official duties or any person dealing with the city concerning such dealings with the city, after first being advised that neither their statements nor any information or evidence derived therefrom will be used against them in a subsequent criminal prosecution other than for perjury or contempt arising from such testimony. The refusal of an officer or employee to answer questions on the condition described in this paragraph shall constitute cause for removal from office or employment or other appropriate penalty.

Every officer or employee of the city shall cooperate fully with the Commissioner and the Inspectors General. Interference with or obstruction of an investigation conducted by the Commissioner or an Inspector General shall constitute cause for removal from office or employment or other appropriate penalty.

Every officer and employee of the city shall have the affirmative obligation to report, directly and without undue delay, to the Commissioner or an Inspector General any and all information concerning conduct which they know or should reasonably know to involve corrupt or other criminal activity or conflict of interest, (1) by another city officer or employee, which concerns his or her office or employment, or (2) by persons dealing with the city, which concerns their dealings with the city. The knowing failure of any officer or employee to report as required above shall constitute cause for removal from office or employment or other appropriate penalty.

4 (#1)

10. According to the above passage, if a city employee has information concerning criminal wrongdoing by her supervisor in his work with a private agency, she should FIRST

    A. speak with her supervisor about the matter
    B. inform the Inspector General of the information she has
    C. explore the matter further to try to uncover more evidence
    D. speak to her co-workers to determine whether her suspicions are valid

10._

11. Of the following, the passage is MOST concerned with

    A. preventing corrupt or other criminal activity or conflicts of interest in city dealings
    B. establishing what constitutes corrupt or criminal activities by city employees
    C. establishing guidelines for removing city employees from office who do not assist the Inspector General
    D. city employees' responsibilities regarding investigations conducted by the Office of the Inspector General

11._

12. Based on the above passage, it is NOT always necessary to report which one of the following to the Inspector General?

    A. a city employee who accepts a gift from a private business
    B. a private agency whose work for the city presents a conflict of interest
    C. a private vendor who offers a city employee special favors if awarded a city contract
    D. a city employee who conducts private business during his city working hours Of the following, the above passage does NOT discuss the type of penally a city employee might receive for

12._

13. Of the following, the above passage does NOT discuss the type of penally a city employee might receive for

    A. intentionally giving misleading answers to questions asked by the Inspector General
    B. criminal actions he committed and which subsequently are uncovered by an investigation of the Inspector General
    C. interfering with an investigation being conducted by the Inspector General
    D. delaying to report corrupt activity to the Inspector General

13._

Questions 14 through 16 are to be answered SOLELY on the basis of the information contained in the following passage.

In 2003, funding for the Older Americans Act programs will be cut by 10% from the 2002 funding levels. There will be 4.6 million dollars less in funds available for congregate and home-delivered meals, employment, and social services for the city's 1.2 million elderly residents. Funding for the Title V Senior Community Services Employment program would be effectively discontinued, resulting in the loss of jobs for 684 elderly persons working in nutrition sites for the elderly, senior centers, day care centers, and hospitals. This job loss would add to the almost 800 jobs in N.Y.C. defunded by the elimination of the Job Opportunity Program Reductions in the Title IIIC Nutrition and Commodity Foods/cash in lieu programs will jeopardize the delivery of over 500,000 congregate and home-delivered meals annually, and the operation of seven senior citizens centers. Title IIIB services, which include home care, escort, shopping, and transportation services, will be spared in 2003 because of the availability of prior year funds, but will be reduced by nearly one million dollars in 2004, causing the interruption of these supportive services for thousands of elderly persons in the city.

5 (#1)

14. According to the information in the above passage, funding cuts for the Title V Senior   14._____
Community Services Employment program would

   A. not affect the availability of home-delivered meals for the elderly
   B. be greater in 2003 because of an overall decline in the city's population
   C. result in the loss of 1,484 jobs for the elderly
   D. impact mostly on the staff assigned to senior centers

15. Based on the information in the above passage, which of the following statements is   15._____
MOST correct?

   A. Funding cuts will affect only a small portion of the city's elderly population
   B. The largest funding cuts will take place in Title IIIC programs.
   C. The Job Opportunity Program will not be affected by cuts in Title IIIB programs.
   D. Funding for Older Americans Act programs will be cut by an additional 10% in
      2004.

16. Based on the information in the above passage, it can be inferred that escort services for   16._____
the elderly will

   A. continue in 2003 but be eliminated in 2004
   B. not be affected in 2004 due to prior year funding
   C. be reduced in 2003 and eliminated in 2004
   D. not be affected in 2003 but reduced in 2004

KEY (CORRECT ANSWERS)

1.	D	9.	C
2.	B	10.	B
3.	B	11.	D
4.	C	12.	A
5.	D	13.	B
6.	D	14.	A
7.	D	15.	C
8.	B	16.	D

REPORT WRITING

EXAMINATION SECTION
TEST 1

DIRECTIONS: Each question or incomplete statement is followed by several suggested answers or completions. Select the one that BEST answers the question or completes the statement. *PRINT THE LETTER OF THE CORRECT ANSWER IN THE SPACE AT THE RIGHT.*

Questions 1-4.

DIRECTIONS: Answer Questions 1 through 4 on the basis of the following report which was prepared by a supervisor for inclusion in his agency's annual report.

Line #	
1	On Oct. 13, I was assigned to study the salaries paid.
2	to clerical employees in various titles by the city and by
3	private industry in the area.
4	In order to get the data I needed, I called Mr. Johnson at
5	the Bureau of the Budget and the payroll officers at X Corp.—
6	a brokerage house, Y Co. —an insurance company, and Z Inc. —
7	a publishing firm. None of them was available and I had to call
8	all of them again the next day.
9	When I finally got the information I needed, I drew up a
10	chart, which is attached. Note that not all of the companies I
11	contacted employed people at all the different levels used in the
12	city service.
13	The conclusions I draw from analyzing this information is
14	as follows: The city's entry-level salary is about average for
15	the region; middle-level salaries are generally higher in the
16	city government plan than in private industry; but salaries at the
17	highest levels in private industry are better than city em-
18	ployees' pay.

1. Which of the following criticisms about the style in which this report is written is MOST valid?
   A. It is too informal.
   B. It is too concise.
   C. It is too choppy.
   D. The syntax is too complex.

1.____

2. Judging from the statements made in the report, the method followed by this employee in performing his research was
   A. *good*; he contacted a representative sample of businesses in the area
   B. *poor*; he should have drawn more definite conclusions
   C. *good*; he was persistent in collecting information
   D. *poor*; he did not make a thorough study

2.____

115

2 (#1)

3. One sentence in this report contains a grammatical error. This sentence begins on line number   3.____
    A. 4   B. 7   C. 10   D. 14

4. The type of information given in this report which should be presented in footnotes or in an appendix is the   4.____
    A. purpose of the study
    B. specifics about the businesses contacted
    C. reference to the chart
    D. conclusions drawn by the author

5. The use of a graph to show statistical data in a report is SUPERIOR to a table because it   5.____
    A. features approximations
    B. emphasizes facts and relationships more dramatically
    C. presents data more accurately
    D. is easily understood by the average reader

6. Of the following, the degree of formality required of a written report in tone is MOST likely to depend on the   6.____
    A. subject matter of the report
    B. frequency of its occurrence
    C. amount of time available for its preparation
    D. audience for whom the report is intended

7. Of the following, a distinguishing characteristic of a written report intended for the head of your agency as compared to a report prepared for a lower-echelon staff member is that the report for the agency head should USUALLY include   7.____
    A. considerably more detail, especially statistical data
    B. the essential details in an abbreviated form
    C. all available source material
    D. an annotated bibliography

8. Assume that you are asked to write a lengthy report for use by the administrator of your agency, the subject of which is "The Impact of Proposed New Data Processing Operation on Line Personnel" in your agency. You decide that the *most* appropriate type of report for you to prepare is an analytical report, including recommendations.   8.____
The MAIN reason for your decision is that
    A. the subject of the report is extremely complex
    B. large sums of money are involved
    C. the report is being prepared for the administrator
    D. you intend to include charts and graphs

3 (#1)

9. Assume that you are preparing a report based on a survey dealing with the attitudes of employees in Division X regarding proposed new changes in compensating employees for working overtime. Three percent of the respondents to the survey voluntarily offer an unfavorable opinion on the method of assigning overtime work, a question not specifically asked of the employees.
On the basis of this information, the MOST appropriate and significant of the following comments for you to make in the report with regard to employees' attitudes on assigning overtime work is that
   A. an insignificant percentage of employees dislike the method of assigning overtime work
   B. three percent of the employees in Division X dislike the method of assigning overtime work
   C. three percent of the sample selected for the survey voiced an unfavorable opinion on the method of assigning overtime work
   D. some employees voluntarily voiced negative feelings about the method of assigning overtime work, making it impossible to determine the extent of this attitude

9.____

10. A supervisor should be able to prepare a report that is well-written and unambiguous.
Of the following sentences that might appear in a report, select the one which communicates MOST clearly the intent of its author.
   A. When your subordinates speak to a group of people, they should be well-informed.
   B. When he asked him to leave, SanMan King told him that he would refuse the request.
   C. Because he is a good worker, Foreman Jefferson assigned Assistant Foreman D'Agostino to replace him.
   D. Each of us is responsible for the actions of our subordinates.

10.____

11. In some reports, especially longer ones, a list of the resources (books, papers, magazines, etc.) used to prepare it is included. This list is called the
   A. accreditation   B. bibliography
   C. summary   D. glossary

11.____

12. Reports are usually divided into several sections, some of which are more necessary than others.
Of the following, the section which is ABSOLUTELY necessary to include in a report is
   A. a table of contents   B. the body
   C. an index   D. a bibliography

12.____

117

4 (#1)

13. Suppose you are writing a report on an interview you have just completed with a particularly hostile applicant.
Which of the following BEST describes what you should include in this report?
    A. What you think caused the applicant's hostile attitude during the interview
    B. Specific examples of the applicant's hostile remarks and behavior
    C. The relevant information uncovered during the interview
    D. A recommendation that the applicant's request be denied because of his hostility

13.____

14. When including recommendations in a report to your supervisor, which of the following is MOST important for you to do?
    A. Provide several alternative courses of action for each recommendation
    B. First present the supporting evidence, then the recommendations
    C. First present the recommendations, then the supporting evidence
    D. Make sure the recommendations arise logically out of the information in the report

14.____

15. It is often necessary that the writer of a report present facts and sufficient arguments to gain acceptance of the points, conclusions, or recommendations set forth in the report.
Of the following, the LEAST advisable step to take in organizing a report, when such argumentation is the important factor, is a(n)
    A. elaborate expression of personal belief
    B. businesslike discussion of the problem as a whole
    C. orderly arrangement of convincing data
    D. reasonable explanation of the primary issues

15.____

16. In some types of reports, visual aids add interest, meaning, and support. They also provide an essential means of effectively communicating the message of the report.
Of the following, the selection of the suitable visual aids to use with a report is LEAST dependent on the
    A. nature and scope of the report
    B. way in which the aid is to be used
    C. aid used in other reports
    D. prospective readers of the report

16.____

17. Visual aids used in a report may be placed either in the text material or in the appendix.
Deciding where to put a chart, table, or any such aid should depend on the
    A. title of the report
    B. purpose of the visual aid
    C. title of the visual aid
    D. length of the report

17.____

18. A report is often revised several times before final preparation and distribution in an effort to make certain the report meets the needs of the situation for which it is designed.
Which of the following is the BEST way for the author to be sure that a report covers the areas he intended?

18.____

5 (#1)

    A. Obtain a coworker's opinion
    B. Compare it with a content checklist
    C. Test it on a subordinate
    D. Check his bibliography

19. In which of the following situations is an oral report preferable to a written report? When a(n)
    A. recommendation is being made for a future plan of action
    B. department head requests immediate information
    C. long-standing policy change is made
    D. analysis of complicated statistical data is involved

19.____

20. When an applicant is approved, the supervisor must fill in standard forms with certain information.
The GREATEST advantage of using standard forms in this situation rather than having the supervisor write the report as he sees fit is that
    A. the report can be acted on quickly
    B. the report can be written without directions from a supervisor
    C. needed information is less likely to be left out of the report
    D. information that is written up this way is more likely to be verified

20.____

21. Assume that it is part of your job to prepare a monthly report for your unit head that eventually goes to the director. The report contains information on the number of applicants you have interviewed that have been approved and the number of applicants you have interviewed that have been turned down.
Errors on such reports are serious because
    A. you are expected to be able to prove how many applicants you have interviewed each month
    B. accurate statistics are needed for effective management of the department
    C. they may not be discovered before the report is transmitted to the director
    D. they may result in loss to the applicants left out of the report

21.____

22. The frequency with which job reports are submitted should depend MAINLY on
    A. how comprehensive the report has to be
    B. the amount of information in the report
    C. the availability of an experienced man to write the report
    D. the importance of changes in the information included in the report

22.____

23. The CHIEF purpose in preparing an outline for a report is usually to insure that
    A. the report will be grammatically correct
    B. every point will be given equal emphasis
    C. principal and secondary points will be properly integrated
    D. the language of the report will be of the same level and include the same technical terms

23.____

6 (#1)

24. The MAIN reason for requiring written job reports is to 24.____
    A. avoid the necessity of oral orders
    B. develop better methods of doing the work
    C. provide a permanent record of what was done
    D. increase the amount of work that can be done

25. Assume you are recommending in a report to your supervisor that a radical 25.____
change in a standard maintenance procedure should be adopted.
Of the following, the MOST important information to be included in this report is
    A. a list of the reasons for making this change
    B. the names of others who favor the change
    C. a complete description of the present procedure
    D. amount of training time needed for the new procedure

KEY (CORRECT ANSWERS)

1.	A		11.	B
2.	D		12.	B
3.	D		13.	C
4.	B		14.	D
5.	B		15.	A
6.	D		16.	C
7.	B		17.	B
8.	A		18.	B
9.	D		19.	B
10.	D		20.	C

21.	B
22.	D
23.	C
24.	C
25.	A

TEST 2

DIRECTIONS: Each question or incomplete statement is followed by several suggested answers or completions. Select the one that BEST answers the question or completes the statement. *PRINT THE LETTER OF THE CORRECT ANSWER IN THE SPACE AT THE RIGHT.*

1. It is often necessary that the writer of a report present facts and sufficient arguments to gain acceptance of the points, conclusions, or recommendations set forth in the report.
   Of the following, the LEAST advisable step to take in organizing a report, when such argumentation is the important factor, is a(n)
   A. elaborate expression of personal belief
   B. businesslike discussion of the problem as a whole
   C. orderly arrangement of convincing data
   D. reasonable explanation of the primary issues

1.____

2. Of the following, the factor which is generally considered to be LEAST characteristic of a good control report is that it
   A. stresses performance that adheres to standard rather than emphasizing the exception
   B. supplies information intended to serve as the basis for corrective action
   C. provides feedback for the planning process
   D. includes data that reflect trends as well as current status

2.____

3. An administrative assistant has been asked by his superior to write a concise, factual report with objective conclusions and recommendations based on facts assembled by other researchers.
   Of the following factors, the administrative assistant should give LEAST consideration to
   A. the educational level of the person or persons for whom the report is being prepared
   B. the use to be made of the report
   C. the complexity of the problem
   D. his own feelings about the importance of the problem

3.____

4. When making a written report, it is often recommended that the findings or conclusions be presented near the beginning of the report.
   Of the following, the MOST important reason for doing this is that it
   A. facilitates organizing the material clearly
   B. assures that all the topics will be covered
   C. avoids unnecessary repetition of ideas
   D. prepares the reader for the facts that will follow

4.____

121

2 (#2)

5. You have been asked to write a report on methods of hiring and training new employees. Your report is going to be about ten pages long.
For the convenience of your readers, a brief summary of your findings should
   A. appear at the beginning of your report
   B. be appended to the report as a postscript
   C. be circulated in a separate memo
   D. be inserted in tabular form in the middle of your report

5.____

6. In preparing a report, the MAIN reason for writing an outline is usually to
   A. help organize thoughts in a logical sequence
   B. provide a guide for the typing of the report
   C. allow the ultimate user to review the report in advance
   D. ensure that the report is being prepared on schedule

6.____

7. The one of the following which is MOST appropriate as a reason for including footnotes in a report is to
   A. correct capitalization   B. delete passages
   C. improve punctuation   D. cite references

7.____

8. A completed formal report may contain all of the following EXCEPT
   A. a synopsis   B. a preface
   C. marginal notes   D. bibliographical references

8.____

9. Of the following, the MAIN use of proofreaders' marks is to
   A. explain corrections to be made
   B. indicate that a manuscript has been read and approved
   C. let the reader know who proofread the report
   D. indicate the format of the report

9.____

10. Informative, readable, and concise reports have been found to observe the following rules:
   Rule I.   Keep the report short and easy to understand
   Rule II.   Vary the length of sentences.
   Rule III. Vary the style of sentences so that, for example, they are not all just subject-verb, subject-verb.
Consider this hospital laboratory report: The experiment was started in January. The apparatus was put together in six weeks. At that time, the synthesizing process was begun. The synthetic chemicals were separated. Then they were used in tests on patients.
Which one of the following choices MOST accurately classifies the above rules into those which are violated by this report ad those which are not?
   A. II is violated, but I and III are not.
   B. III is violated, but I and II are not.
   C. II and III are violated, but I is not.
   D. I, II, and III are violated,

10.____

3 (#2)

Questions 11-13.

DIRECTIONS: Questions 11 through 13 are based on the following example of a report. The report consists of eight numbered sentences, some of which are not consistent with the principles of good report writing.

(1) I interviewed Mrs. Loretta Crawford in Room 424 of County Hospital. (2) She had collapsed on the street and been brought into emergency. (3) She is an attractive woman with many friends judging by the cards she had received. (4) She did not know what her husband's last job had been, or what their present income was. (5) The first thing that Mrs. Crawford said was that she had never worked and that her husband was presently unemployed. (6) She did not know if they had any medical coverage or if they could pay the bill. (7) She said that her husband could not be reached by telephone but that he would be in to see her that afternoon. (8) I left word at the nursing station to be called when he arrived.

11.   A good report should be arranged in logical order.   11._____
      Which of the following sentences from the report does NOT appear in its proper sequence in the report?
      A. 1   B. 4   C. 7   D. 8

12.   Only material that is relevant to the main thought of a report should be included.   12._____
      Which of the following sentences from the report contains material which is LEAST relevant to this report? Sentence
      A. 3   B. 4   C. 6   D. 8

13.   Reports should include all essential information.   13._____
      Of the following, the MOST important fact that is missing from this report is:
      A. Who was involved in the interview
      B. What was discovered at the interview
      C. When the interview took place
      D. Where the interview took place

Questions 14-15.

DIRECTIONS: Each of Questions 14 and 15 consists of four numbered sentences which constitute a paragraph in a report. They are not in the right order. Choose the numbered arrangement appearing after letter A, B, C, or D which is MOST logical and which BEST expresses the thought of the paragraph.

14.   I.   Congress made the commitment explicit in the Housing Act of 1949,   14._____
             establishing as a national goal the realization of a decent home and
             suitable environment for every American family.
      II.   The result has been that the goal of decent home and suitable
             environment is still as far distant as ever for the disadvantaged urban
             family
      III.   In spite of this action by Congress, federal housing programs have
             continued to be fragmented and grossly under-funded.
      IV.   The passage of the National Housing Act signaled a new federal
             commitment to provide housing for the nation's citizens.

4 (#2)

The CORRECT answer is:
A. I, IV, III, II   B. IV, I, III, II   C. IV, I, III, II   D. II, IV, I, III

15.   I. The greater expense does not necessarily involve "exploitation," but it is often perceived as exploitative and unfair by those who are aware of the price differences involved, but unaware of operating costs.
  II. Ghetto residents believe they are "exploited" by local merchants, and evidence substantiates some of these beliefs.
  III. However, stores in low-income areas were more likely to be small independents, which could not achieve the economies available to supermarket chains and were, therefore, more likely to charge higher prices, and the customers were more likely to buy smaller-sized packages which are more expensive per unit of measure.
  IV. A study conducted in one city showed that distinctly higher prices were charged for goods sold in ghetto stores than in other areas.

    The CORRECT answer is:
    A. IV, II, I, III   B. IV, I, III, II   C. II, IV, III, I   D. II, III, IV, I

16. In organizing data to be presented in a formal report, the FIRST of the following steps should be
    A. determining the conclusions to be drawn
    B. establishing the time sequence of the data
    C. sorting and arranging like data into groups
    D. evaluating how consistently the data support the recommendations

17. All reports should be prepared with at least one copy so that
    A. there is one copy for your file
    B. there is a copy for your supervisor
    C. the report can be sent to more than one person
    D. the person getting the report can forward a copy to someone else

18. Before turning in a report of an investigation he has made, a supervisor discovers some additional information he did not include in this report. Whether he rewrites this report to include this additional information should PRIMARILY depend on the
    A. importance of the report itself
    B. number of people who will eventually review this report
    C. established policy covering the subject matter of the report
    D. bearing this new information has on the conclusions of the report

5 (#2)

KEY (CORRECT ANSWERS)

1.	A	11.	B
2.	A	12.	A
3.	D	13.	C
4.	D	14.	B
5.	A	15.	C
6.	A	16.	C
7.	D	17.	A
8.	C	18.	D
9.	A		
10.	C		

DOCUMENTS AND FORMS
PREPARING WRITTEN MATERIALS
EXAMINATION SECTION
TEST 1

DIRECTIONS: Each question or incomplete statement is followed by several suggested answers or completions. Select the one that BEST answers the question or completes the statement. *PRINT THE LETTER OF THE CORRECT ANSWER IN THE SPACE AT THE RIGHT.*

1. Of the following forms, the one in which horizontal lines may BEST be omitted is one

   A. that is to be filled in by hand
   B. that is to be filled in by typewriter
   C. which requires many fill-ins
   D. with little room for fill-ins

1.____

2. A certain form letter starts with the words *Dear Mr.* followed by a blank space. The MAJOR shortcoming in this is that

   A. salutations should not be placed on form letters
   B. *Gentlemen:* is preferable in a formal business letter
   C. the name will have to be typed in
   D. this salutation may be inappropriate

2.____

3. *Form paragraphs* may BEST be defined as

   A. block-style paragraphs
   B. paragraphs on a form
   C. paragraphs within a form letter
   D. standardized paragraphs used in correspondence

3.____

4. In general, the CHIEF economy of using multicopy forms is in

   A. the paper on which the form is printed
   B. printing the form
   C. employee time
   D. carbon paper

4.____

5. Suppose your supervisor has asked you to develop a form to record certain information needed.
   The FIRST thing you should do is to

   A. determine the type of data that will be recorded repeatedly so that it can be pre-printed
   B. study the relationship of the form to the job to be accomplished so that the form can be planned
   C. determine the information that will be recorded in the same place on each copy of the form so that it can be used as a check
   D. find out who will be responsible for supplying the information so that space can be provided for their signatures

5.____

127

2 (#1)

6. Which of the following is MOST likely to reduce the volume of paperwork in a unit responsible for preparing a large number of reports?

    A. Changing the office layout so that there will be a minimum of backtracking and delay
    B. Acquiring additional adding and calculating machines
    C. Consolidating some of the reports
    D. Inaugurating a *records retention* policy to reduce the length of time office papers are retained

6._

7. Of the following basic guides to effective letter writing, which one would NOT be recommended as a way of improving the quality of business letters?

    A. Use emphatic phrases like *close proximity* and *first and foremost* to round out sentences.
    B. Break up complicated sentences by making short sentences out of dependent clauses.
    C. Replace old-fashioned phrases like *enclosed please find* and *recent date* with a more direct approach.
    D. Personalize letters by using your reader's name at least once in the body of the message.

7._

8. Suppose that you must write a reply letter to a citizen's request for a certain pamphlet printed by your agency. The pamphlet is temporarily unavailable but a new supply will be arriving by December 8 or 9.
Of the following four sentences, which one expresses the MOST positive business letter writing approach?

    A. We cannot send the materials you requested until after December 8.
    B. May we assure you that the materials you requested will be sent as quickly as possible.
    C. We will be sending the materials you requested as soon as our supply is replenished.
    D. We will mail the materials you requested on or shortly after December 8.

8._

9. Using form letters in business correspondence is LEAST effective when

    A. answering letters on a frequently recurring subject
    B. giving the same information to many addresses
    C. the recipient is only interested in the routine information contained in the form letter
    D. a reply must be keyed to the individual requirements of the intended reader

9._

10. The ability to write memos and letters is very important in clerical and administrative work. Methodical planning of a reply letter usually involves the following basic steps which are arranged in random order:

    I. Determine the purpose of the letter you are about to write.
    II. Make an outline of what information your reply letter should contain.
    III. Read carefully the letter to be answered to find out its main points.
    IV. Assemble the facts to be included in your reply letter.
    V. Visualize your intended reader and adapt your letter writing style to him.

If the above numbered steps were arranged in their proper logical order, the one which would be THIRD in the sequence is

    A. II   B. III   C. IV   D. V

10._

3 (#1)

11. Generally, the frequency with which reports are to be submitted or the length of the interval which they cover should depend MAINLY on the   11._____

    A. amount of time needed to prepare the reports
    B. degree of comprehensiveness required in the reports
    C. availability of the data to be included in the reports
    D. extent of the variations in the data with the passage of time

12. The objectiveness of a report is its unbiased presentation of the facts.   12._____
If this is so, which of the following reports listed below is likely to be the MOST objective?

    A. The Best Use of an Electronic Computer in Department Z
    B. The Case for Raising the Salaries of Employees in Department A
    C. Quarterly Summary of Production in the Duplicating Unit of Department Y
    D. Recommendation to Terminate Employee X's Services Because of Misconduct

13. Of the following, the MOST effective report writing style is usually characterized by   13._____

    A. covering all the main ideas in the same paragraph
    B. presenting each significant point in a new paragraph
    C. placing the least important points before the most important points
    D. giving all points equal emphasis throughout the report

14. Of the following, which factor is COMMON to all types of reports?   14._____

    A. Presentation of information
    B. Interpretation of findings
    C. Chronological ordering of the information
    D. Presentation of conclusions and recommendations

15. When writing a report, the one of the following which you should do FIRST is   15._____

    A. set up a logical work schedule
    B. determine your objectives in writing the report
    C. select your statistical material
    D. obtain the necessary data from the files

16. Good report writing utilizes, where possible, the use of table of contents, clear titles and sub-titles, well-labeled tables and figures, and good summaries in prominent places. These features in a report are MOST helpful in   16._____

    A. saving the reader's time
    B. emphasizing objectivity
    C. providing a basic reference tool
    D. forming a basis for future action

17. The one of the following which BEST describes a periodic report is that it   17._____

    A. provides a record of accomplishments for a given time span and a comparison with similar time spans in the past
    B. covers the progress made in a project that has been postponed
    C. integrates, summarizes, and perhaps interprets published data on technical or scientific material
    D. describes a decision, advocates a policy or action, and presents facts in support of the writer's position

4 (#1)

18. The PRIMARY purpose of including pictorial illustrations in a formal report is usually to   18.

    A. amplify information which has been adequately treated verbally
    B. present details that are difficult to describe verbally
    C. provide the reader with a pleasant, momentary distraction
    D. present supplementary information incidental to the main ideas developed in the report

19. Of the following, which is usually the MOST important guideline in writing business letters?   19.
A letter should be

    A. Neat
    B. Written in a formalized style
    C. Written in clear language intelligible to the reader
    D. Written in the past tense

20. Suppose you are asked to edit a policy statement. You note that personal pronouns like *you, we,* and *I* are used freely.   20.
Which of the following statements BEST applies to this use of personal pronouns?

    A. It is proper usage because written business language should not be different from carefully spoken business language.
    B. It requires correction because it is ungrammatical.
    C. It is proper because it is clearer and has a warmer tone.
    D. It requires correction because policies should be expressed in an impersonal manner.

21. Good business letters are coherent.   21.
To be coherent means to

    A. keep only one unifying idea in the message
    B. present the total message
    C. use simple, direct words for the message
    D. tie together the various ideas in the message

22. A functional forms file is a collection of forms which are grouped by   22.

    A. purpose   B. department   C. title   D. subject

23. All of the following are reasons to consult a records retention schedule except one.   23.
Which one is that?
To determine

    A. Whether something should be filed
    B. How long something should stay in file
    C. Who should be assigned to filing
    D. When something on file should be destroyed

5 (#1)

24. A secretary is MOST likely to employ a form letter when   24.____

    A. an answer is not required
    B. the same information must be repeated from letter to letter
    C. there is not enough information to write a detailed reply
    D. varied correspondence must be sent out quickly

25. Of the following, the BASIC intent of naming a form is to provide the means to   25.____

    A. code those factors recorded on each form
    B. describe the use of the form
    C. index each form
    D. call attention to specific sections within each form

KEY (CORRECT ANSWERS)

1.	B		11.	D
2.	D		12.	C
3.	D		13.	B
4.	C		14.	A
5.	B		15.	B
6.	C		16.	A,C
7.	A		17.	A
8.	D		18.	B
9.	D		19.	C
10.	A		20.	D

21.	D
22.	A
23.	C
24.	B
25.	B

TEST 2

DIRECTIONS: Each question or incomplete statement is followed by several suggested answers or completions. Select the one that BEST answers the question or completes the statement. *PRINT THE LETTER OF THE CORRECT ANSWER IN THE SPACE AT THE RIGHT.*

1. Assume that you are assigned the task of reducing the time and costs involved in completing a form that is frequently used in your agency. After analyzing the matter, you decide to reduce the writing requirements of the form through the use of ballot boxes and preprinted data.
If exact copy-to-copy registration of this form is necessary, it is MOST advisable to

    A. vary the sizes of the ballot boxes
    B. stagger the ballot boxes
    C. place the ballot boxes as close together as possible
    D. have the ballot boxes follow the captions

2. To overcome problems that are involved in the use of cut-sheet and padded forms, specialty forms have been developed. Normally, these forms are commercially manufactured rather than produced in-plant. Before designing a form as a specialty form, however, you should be assured that certain factors are present.
Which one of the following factors deserve LEAST consideration?

    A. The form is to be used in quantities of 5,000 or more annually.
    B. The forms will be prepared on equipment using either a pinfeed device or pressure rollers for continuous feed-through.
    C. Two or more copies of the form set must be held together for further processing subsequent to the initial distribution of the form set.
    D. Copies of the form will be identical, and no items of data will be selectively eliminated from one or more copies of the form.

3. Although a well-planned form should require little explanation as to its completion, there are many occasions when the analyst will find it necessary to include instructions on the form to assure that the person completing it does so correctly.
With respect to such instructions, it is usually considered to be LEAST appropriate to place them

    A. in footnotes at the bottom of the form
    B. following the spaces to be completed
    C. directly under the form's title
    D. on the front of the form

4. One of the basic data-arrangement methods used in forms design is the *on-line* method. When this method is used, captions appear on the same line as the space provided for entry of the variable data.
This arrangement is NOT recommended because it

    A. forces the typist to make use of the typewriter's tab stops, thus increasing processing time
    B. wastes horizontal space since the caption appears on the writing line
    C. tends to make the variable data become more dominant than the captions
    D. increases the form's processing time by requiring the typist to continually roll the platen back and forth to expose the caption

2 (#2)

5. Of the following, the BEST reason for using form letters in correspondence is that they are   5.____

    A. concise and businesslike
    B. impersonal in tone
    C. uniform in appearance
    D. economical for large mailings

6. Of the following, the MOST important reason to sort large volumes of documents before filing is that sorting   6.____

    A. decreases the need for cross-referencing
    B. eliminates the need to keep the files up to date
    C. prevents overcrowding of the file drawers
    D. saves time and energy in filing

7. To overcome the manual collation problem, forms are frequently padded.
Of the following statements which relate to this type of packaging, select the one that is MOST accurate.   7.____

    A. Typewritten forms which are prepared as padded forms are more efficient than all other packaging.
    B. Padded forms are best suited for handwritten forms.
    C. It is difficult for a printer to pad form copies of different colors.
    D. Registration problems increase when cut-sheet forms are padded.

8. Most forms are cut from a standard mill sheet of paper. This is the size on which forms dealers base their prices. Since an agency is paying for a full-size sheet of paper, it is the responsibility of the analyst to design forms so that as many as possible may be cut from the sheet without waste.
Of the following sizes, select the one that will cut from a standard mill sheet with the GREATEST waste and should, therefore, be avoided if possible.   8.____

    A. 4" x 6"   B. 5" x 8"   C. 9" x 12"   D. $8\frac{1}{2}$" x 14"

9. Assume that the work in your department involves the use of many technical terms.
In such a situation, when you are answering inquiries from the general public, it would usually be BEST to   9.____

    A. use simple language and avoid the technical terms
    B. use the technical terms whenever possible
    C. use technical terms freely, but explain each term in parentheses
    D. apologize if you are forced to use a technical term

10. You are answering a letter that was written on the letterhead of the ABC Company and signed by James H. Block, Treasurer.
What is usually considered to be the CORRECT salutation to use in your reply?
Dear   10.____

    A. ABC Company: B. Sirs:
    C. Mr. Block: D. Mr. Treasurer:

133

3 (#2)

11. Assume that one of your duties is to handle routine letters of inquiry from the public. The one of the following which is usually considered to be MOST desirable in replying to such a letter is a

    A. detailed answer handwritten on the original letter of inquiry
    B. phone call since you can cover details more easily over the phone than in a letter
    C. short letter giving the specific information requested
    D. long letter discussing all possible aspects of the questions raised

11.___

12. The CHIEF reason for dividing a letter into paragraphs is to

    A. make the message clear to the reader by starting a new paragraph for each new topic
    B. make a short letter occupy as much of the page as possible
    C. keep the reader's attention by providing a pause from time to time
    D. make the letter look neat and businesslike

12.___

13. An *Attention* line is used in correspondence to

    A. indicate to the person receiving the correspondence that it contains an enclosure
    B. direct correspondence addressed to an organization to a particular individual within the organization
    C. greet the recipient of the correspondence
    D. highlight the main concern of the correspondence

13.___

14. In deciding upon the advisability of recording certain information on a regular basis, the MOST important consideration is:

    A. How much will it cost?
    B. Is it necessary?
    C. Is space available for keeping additional records?
    D. Will it fit into the work pattern?

14.___

15. Instructions for filling out simple forms should USUALLY appear

    A. at the bottom of the form
    B. on a separate sheet of instructions
    C. on the reverse side of the form
    D. with the items to which they refer

15.___

16. Each new form should be given a number PRIMARILY because

    A. it provides a means of easy reference
    B. names are not sufficiently descriptive
    C. numbering forms is common government practice
    D. numbers are more suitable for automatic data processing

16.___

17. Of the following, the MOST important features of an effective business letter are

    A. introduction and conclusion
    B. punctuation and paragraphing
    C. simplicity and clarity
    D. style and organization

17.___

4 (#2)

18. When recording receipt of purchases of equipment, the one of the following which is usually LEAST important is   18.____

    A. identification of the item
    B. name of the vendor
    C. quantity of the item
    D. weight of the item

19. In deciding which data should be collected for permanent records, the MOST important consideration is the   19.____

    A. amount of data available
    B. ease of processing the different types of data
    C. type of record-keeping system involved
    D. use to which such data may be put

20. In a certain filing system, documents are consecutively numbered as they are filed, a register is maintained of such consecutively numbered documents, and a record is kept of the number of each document removed from the files and its destination.
This system will NOT help in   20.____

    A. finding the present whereabouts of a particular document
    B. proving the accuracy of the data recorded on a certain document
    C. indicating whether observed existing documents were ever filed
    D. locating a desired document without knowing what its contents are

21. The inside address in a business letter indicates to whom the letter is to be sent.
Of the following, the MOST important reason why a letter should contain the inside address is that the inside address   21.____

    A. gives the letter a personal, friendly tone
    B. simplifies the work of dictation and transcription
    C. gives the letter a balanced appearance
    D. identifies the addressee when the envelope containing the letter is discarded

22. The appearance of a business letter should make a favorable first impression on the person to whom the letter is sent.
In order to make such an impression, it is LEAST important that the   22.____

    A. letter be centered on the page
    B. margins be as even as possible
    C. letter make a neat appearance
    D. paragraphs be of the same length

23. A typed rough draft of a report should be double-spaced and should have wide margins PRIMARILY in order to   23.____

    A. estimate the number of pages the report will contain
    B. allow space for making corrections in the report
    C. determine whether the report is well-organized
    D. make the report easy to read

135

5 (#2)

24. Suppose that you are assigned to make a number of original typewritten copies of a   24.__
printed report. In doing this assignment, you type the first copy from the printed report
and then type each subsequent copy from the last one you prepared.
You could be MOST certain that there were no errors made in the copies if you found
no errors when comparing the

    A. printed report with any one of the copies
    B. first copy with the printed report
    C. last copy with the printed report
    D. first copy with the last copy

25. Before typing on more than one copy of a printed form, the one of the following which you   25.__
should do FIRST is to

    A. align the type so that the tails of the longer letters will rest on the lines printed on
the form
    B. check the alignment of the copies of the forms by holding them up to the light
    C. insert the carbon paper into the typewriter and then insert the copies of the form
    D. insert the copies of the form into the typewriter and then insert the carbon paper

---

KEY (CORRECT ANSWERS)

1.	B		11.	C
2.	D		12.	A
3.	A		13.	B
4.	B		14.	B
5.	D		15.	D
6.	D		16.	A
7.	B		17.	C
8.	C		18.	D
9.	A		19.	D
10.	C		20.	B

21.	D
22.	D
23.	B
24.	C
25.	B

TEST 3

DIRECTIONS: Each question or incomplete statement is followed by several suggested answers or completions. Select the one that BEST answers the question or completes the statement. *PRINT THE LETTER OF THE CORRECT ANSWER IN THE SPACE AT THE RIGHT.*

1. The supervisor who makes a special point of using long words in preparing written reports is, in general, PROBABLY being

   A. *unwise* because a written report should be factual and accurate
   B. *unwise* because simplicity in a report is usually desirable
   C. *wise* because the written report will become a permanent record
   D. *wise* because with long words he can use the right emphasis in his report

   1.____

2. Before you turn in a report you have written of an investigation that you made, you dis-cover some additional information that you didn't know about before.
   Whether or not you rewrite your report to include this additional information should depend MAINLY on the

   A. amount of time left in which to submit the report
   B. effect this information will have on the conclusions of the report
   C. number of changes that you will have to make in your original report
   D. possibility of turning in a supplementary report later

   2.____

3. When an applicant is approved for public assistance, the supervising clerk must fill in standard forms with certain information.
   The GREATEST advantage of using standard forms in this situation rather than having the supervising clerk write the report as he sees fit is that

   A. the report can be acted on quickly
   B. the report can be written without directions from a supervisor
   C. needed information is less likely to be left out of the report
   D. information that is written up this way is more likely to be verified

   3.____

4. In some types of reports, visual aids add interest, meaning, and support. They also pro-vide an essential means of effectively communicating the message of the report.
   Of the following, the selection of the suitable visual aids to use with a report is LEAST dependent on the

   A. nature and scope of the report
   B. way in which the aid is to be used
   C. aids used in other reports
   D. prospective readers of the report

   4.____

5. A report is often revised several times before final preparation and distribution in an effort to make certain the report meets the needs of the situation for which it is designed.
   Which of the following is the BEST way for the author to be sure that a report covers the areas he intended?

   A. Obtain a co-worker's opinion
   B. Compare it with a content checklist
   C. Test it on a subordinate
   D. Check his bibliography

   5.____

137

2 (#3)

6. Visual aids used in a report may be placed either in the text material or in the appendix. Deciding where to put a chart, table, or any such aid should depend on the

    A. title of the report
    B. purpose of the visual aid
    C. title of the visual aid
    D. length of the report

7. In which of the following situations is an oral report PREFERABLE to a written report? When a(n)

    A. recommendation is being made for a future plan of action
    B. department head requests immediate information
    C. long-standing policy change is made
    D. analysis of complicated statistical data is involved

8. All of the following rules will aid in producing clarity in report writing EXCEPT:

    A. Give specific details or examples, if possible
    B. Keep related words close together in each sentence
    C. Present information in sequential order
    D. Put several thoughts or ideas in each paragraph

9. When preparing a long report on a study prepared for your superior, the one of the following which should usually come FIRST in your report is a(n)

    A. brief description of the working procedure followed in your study
    B. review of the background conditions leading to the study
    C. summary of your conclusions
    D. outline of suggested procedures for implementing the report

10. The MAIN function of a research report is usually to

    A. convince the reader of the adequacy of the research
    B. report as expeditiously as possible what was done, why it was done, the results, and the conclusions
    C. contribute to the body of scientific knowledge
    D. substantiate an a priori conclusion by presenting a set of persuasive quantitative data

11. Words in a sentence must be arranged properly to make sure that the intended meaning of the sentence is clear. The sentence below that does NOT make sense because a clause has been separated from the word on which its meaning depends is:

    A. To be a good writer, clarity is necessary.
    B. To be a good writer, you must write clearly.
    C. You must write clearly to be a good writer.
    D. Clarity is necessary to good writing.

12. The use of a graph to show statistical data in a report is SUPERIOR to a table because it

    A. emphasizes approximations
    B. emphasizes facts and relationships more dramatically
    C. presents data more accurately
    D. is easily understood by the average reader

138

3 (#3)

13. Of the following, the degree of formality required of a written report prepared by a labor   13.____
    relations specialist is MOST likely to depend on the

    A. subject matter of the report
    B. frequency of its occurrence
    C. amount of time available for its preparation
    D. audience for whom the report is intended

14. Of the following, a DISTINGUISHING characteristic of a written report intended for the   14.____
    head of your agency as compared to a report prepared for a lower-echelon staff member
    is that the report for the agency should usually include

    A. considerably more detail, especially statistical data
    B. the essential details in an abbreviated form
    C. all available source material
    D. an annotated bibliography

15. Assume that you are asked to write a lengthy report for use by the administrator of your   15.____
    agency, the subject of which is *The Impact of Proposed New Data Processing Opera-
    tions on Line Personnel* in your agency. You decide that the most appropriate type of
    report for you to prepare is an analytical report, including recommendations.
    The MAIN reason for your decision is that

    A. the subject of the report is extremely complex
    B. large sums of money are involved
    C. the report is being prepared for the administrator
    D. you intend to include charts and graphs

16. Assume that you are preparing a report based on a survey dealing with the attitudes of   16.____
    employees in Division X regarding proposed new changes in compensating employees
    for working overtime. Three percent of the respondents to the survey voluntarily offer an
    unfavorable opinion on the method of assigning overtime work, a question not specifi-
    cally asked of the employees.
    On the basis of this information, the MOST appropriate and significant of the following
    comments for you to make in the report with regard to employees' attitudes on assign-
    ing overtime work is that

    A. an insignificant percentage of employees dislike the method of assigning overtime
       work
    B. three percent of the employees in Division X dislike the method of assigning over-
       time work
    C. three percent of the sample selected for the survey voiced an unfavorable opinion
       on the method of assigning overtime work
    D. some employees voluntarily voiced negative feelings about the method of assign-
       ing overtime work, making it impossible to determine the extent of this attitude

17. Four parts of a survey report are listed below, not necessarily in their proper order: 17.____
       I.   Body of report
       II. Synopsis of report
       III. Letter of transmittal
       IV. Conclusions
    Which one of the following represents the BEST sequence for inclusion of these parts
    in a report?

    A. III, IV, I, II   B. II, I, III, IV   C. III, II, I, IV   D. I, III, IV, II

4 (#3)

18. Of the following, the MOST important value of a good report is that it   18.___

   A. reflects credit upon the person who submitted the report
   B. provides good reference material
   C. expedites official business
   D. expresses the need for official action

19. The MOST important requirement in report writing is   19.___

   A. promptness in turning in reports
   B. length
   C. grammatical construction
   D. accuracy

20. You have discovered an error in your report submitted to the main office.   20.___
    You should

   A. wait until the error is discovered in the main office and then correct it
   B. go directly to the supervisor in the main office after working hours and ask him
      unofficially to correct the answer
   C. notify the main office immediately so that the error can be corrected if necessary
   D. do nothing since it is possible that one error will have little effect on the total report

21. When you determine the methods of emphasis you will use in typing the titles, headings,   21.___
    and subheadings of a report, the one of the following which it is MOST important to keep
    in mind is that

   A. all headings of the same rank should be typed in the same way
   B. all headings should be typed in the single style which is most pleasing to the eye
   C. headings should not take up more than one-third of the page width
   D. only one method should be used for all headings, whatever their rank

22. Proper division of a letter into paragraphs requires that the writer of business letters   22.___
    should, as much as possible, be sure that

   A. each paragraph is short
   B. each paragraph develops discussion of just one topic
   C. each paragraph repeats the theme of the total message
   D. there are at least two paragraphs for every message

23. An editor is given a letter with this initial paragraph: 23.___
    *We have received your letter, which we read with interest, and we are happy to
    respond to your question. In fact, we talked with several people in our office to get
    ideas to send to you.*
    Which of the following is it MOST reasonable for the editor to conclude?
    The paragraph is

   A. concise
   B. communicating something of value
   C. unnecessary
   D. coherent

140

5 (#3)

24. In preparing a report that includes several tables, if not otherwise instructed, the typist should MOST properly include a list of tables   24._____

    A.   in the introductory part of the report
    B.   at the end of each chapter in the body of the report
    C.   in the supplementary part of the report as an appendix
    D.   in the supplementary part of the report as a part of the index

25. You have been asked to write a report on methods of hiring and training new employees. Your report is going to be about ten pages long.   25._____
For the convenience of your readers, a brief summary of your findings should

    A.   appear at the beginning of your report
    B.   be appended to the report as a postscript
    C.   be circulated in a separate memo
    D.   be inserted in tabular form in the middle of your report

26. A new student program is being set up for which certain new forms will be needed. You have been asked to design these forms.   26._____
Of the following, the FIRST step you should take in planning the forms is

    A.   finding out the exact purpose for which each form will be used
    B.   deciding what size of paper should be used for each form
    C.   determining whether multiple copies will be needed for any of the forms
    D.   setting up a new filing system to handle the new forms

27. Many government agencies require the approval by a central forms control unit of the design and reproduction of new office forms.   27._____
The one of the following results of this procedure that is a DISADVANTAGE is that requiring prior approval of a central forms control unit usually

    A.   limits the distribution of forms to those offices with justifiable reasons for receiving them
    B.   permits checking whether existing forms or modifications of them are in line with current agency needs
    C.   encourages reliance on only the central office to set up all additional forms when needed
    D.   provides for someone with a specialized knowledge of forms design to review and criticize new and revised forms

28. Suppose that you are assigned to prepare a form from which certain information will be posted in a ledger.   28._____
It would be MOST helpful to the person posting the information in the ledger if, in designing the form, you were to

    A.   use the same color paper for both the form and the ledger
    B.   make the form the same size as the pages of the ledger
    C.   have the information on the form in the same order as that used in the ledger
    D.   include in the form a box which is to be initialed when the data on the form have been posted in the ledger

141

6 (#3)

29. In the effective design of office forms, the FIRST step to take is to 29.

    A. decide what information should be included
    B. decide the purpose for which the form will be used
    C. identify the form by name and number
    D. identify the employees who will be using the form

30. Some designers of office forms prefer to locate the instructions on how to fill out the form 30.
at the bottom of it.
The MOST logical objection to placing such instructions at the bottom of the form is
that

    A. instructions at the bottom require an excess of space
    B. all form instructions should be outlined with a separate paragraph
    C. the form may be partly filled out before the instructions are seen
    D. the bottom of the form should be reserved only for authorization and signature

---

KEY (CORRECT ANSWERS)

1.	B	11.	A	21.	A
2.	B	12.	B	22.	B
3.	C	13.	D	23.	C
4.	C	14.	B	24.	A
5.	B	15.	A	25.	A
6.	B	16.	D	26.	A
7.	B	17.	C	27.	C
8.	D	18.	C	28.	C
9.	C	19.	D	29.	B
10.	B	20.	C	30.	C

ENGLISH GRAMMAR AND USAGE
EXAMINATION SECTION
TEST 1

DIRECTIONS: In the passages that follow, certain words and phrases are underlined and numbered. In each question, you will find alternatives for each underlined part. You are to choose the one that BEST expresses the idea, makes the statement appropriate for standard written English, or is worded MOST consistently with the style and tone of the passage as a whole. Choose the alternative you consider BEST and write the letter in the space at the right. If you think the original version is BEST, choose NO CHANGE. Read each passage through once before you begin to answer the questions that accompany it. You cannot determine most answers without reading several sentences beyond the phrase in question. Be sure that you have read far enough ahead each time you choose an alternative.

Questions 1-14.

DIRECTIONS: Questions 1 through 14 are based on the following passage.

Modern filmmaking <u>had began</u> in Paris in 1895 with the work of the Lumiere brothers.
1

Using their <u>invention, the Cinématographe,</u> the Lumières were able to photograph, print,
2

and project moving pictures onto a screen. Their films showed <u>actual occurrences. A</u> train
3

approaching a station, people a factory, workers demolishing a wall.

These early films had neither plot nor sound. But another Frenchman, Georges M<u>éliès,</u>

soon incorporated plot lines <u>into</u> his films. And with his attempts to draw upon the potential of
4

film to create fantasy <u>worlds.</u> Méliès also <u>was an early pioneer from</u> special film effects. Edwin
5   6

Porter, an American filmmaker, took Méliès emphasis on narrative one step further. Believing

<u>that, continuity of shots</u> was of primary importance in filmmaking, Porter connected
7

<u>images to present,</u> a sustained action. His GREAT TRAIN ROBBERY of 1903 opened a new
8

era in film.

<u>Because</u> film was still considered <u>as</u> *low* entertainment in early twentieth century America,
9   10

it was on its way to becoming a respected art form. Beginning in 1908, the American director

D.W. Griffith discovered and explored techniques to make film a more expressive medium.

2 (#1)

With his technical contributions, <u>as well as</u> his attempts to develop the intellectual and moral
                                        11
potential of film, Griffith helped build a solid foundation for the industry.

Thirty years after the Lumière brothers' first show, sound <u>had yet been</u> added to the
  12   13
movies. Finally, in 1927, Hollywood produced its first *talkie*, THE JAZZ SINGER. With sound,

modern film <u>coming</u> of age.
               14

1. A. NO CHANGE   B. begun   1.____
   C. began   D. had some beginnings

2. A. NO CHANGE   B. invention—the Cinématographe   2.____
   C. invention, the Cinématgraphe—   D. invention, the Cinématographe

3. A. NO CHANGE   B. actually occurrences, a   3.____
   C. actually occurrences—a   D. actual occurrences: a

4. A. NO CHANGE   B. about   4.____
   C. with   D. to

5. A. NO CHANGE   B. worlds   5.____
   C. worlds' and   D. worlds and

6. A. NO CHANGE   B. pioneered   6.____
   C. pioneered the beginnings of   D. pioneered the early beginnings of

7. A. NO CHANGE   B. that continuity of shots   7.____
   C. that, continuity of shots,   D. that continuity of shots

8. A. NO CHANGE   B. images to present   8.____
   C. that, continuity of shots   D. that continuity of shots

9. A. NO CHANGE   9.____
   B. (Begin new paragraph) in view of the fact that
   C. (Begin new paragraph) Although
   D. Do NOT begin new paragraph) Since

10. A. NO CHANGE   B. as if it were   10.____
    C. like it was   D. OMIT the underlined portion

11. A. NO CHANGE   B. similar to   11.____
    C. similar with   D. like with

3 (#1)

12. A. NO CHANGE
    B. (Begin new paragraph) Consequently, thirty
    C. (Do NOT begin new paragraph) Therefore, thirty
    D. (Do NOT begin new paragraph) As a consequence, thirty

12.____

13. A. NO CHANGE
    B. (Begin new paragraph) Consequently, thirty
    C. (No NOT begin new paragraph) Therefore, thirty
    D. (Do NOT begin new paragraph As a consequence, thirty

13.____

14. A. NO CHANGE   B. comes
    C. came   D. had came

14.____

Questions 15-22.

DIRECTIONS: Questions 15 through 22 are based on the following passage.

One of the most awesome forces in nature is the tsunami, or tidal wave. A

tsunami—the word is Japanese for harbor wave, can generate the destructive power of many
                15
atomic bombs.

Tsunamis usually appear in a series of four or five waves about fifteen minutes apart.
        16
They begin deep in the ocean, gather remarkable speed as they travel, and cover great

instances. The wave triggered by the explosion of Krakatoa in 1883 circled the world in three

days.

Tsunamis being known to sink large ships at sea, they are most dangerous when they
        17
reach land. Close to shore, an oncoming tsunami is forced upward and skyward, perhaps as
                                                                    18
high as 100 feet. This combination of height and speed accounts for the tsunami's great power.

That *tsunami* is a Japanese word is no accident, due to the fact that no nation
                                                    19
frequently has been so visited by giant waves as Japan. Tsunamis reach that country regularly,
    20   21
and with devastating consequences. One Japanese tsunami flattened several towns in

1896, also killed 27,000 people. The 2011 tsunami caused similar loss of life as well as untold
        22
damage from nuclear radiation.

145

4 (#1)

15. A. NO CHANGE
     B. tsunami, the word is Japanese for harbor wave—
     C. tsunami—the word is Japanese for harbor wave—
     D. tsunami—the word being Japanese for harbor wave,

15.____

16. A. NO CHANGE
     B. (Begin new paragraph) Consequently, tsunamis
     C. (Do NOT begin new paragraph) Tsunamis consequently
     D. (Do NOT begin new paragraph) Yet, tsunamis

16.____

17. A. NO CHANGE   B. Because tsunamis have been
     C. Although tsunamis have been   D. Tsunamis have been

17.____

18. A. NO CHANGE   B. upward to the sky,
     C. upward in the sky   D. upward,

18.____

19. A. NO CHANGE
     B. when one takes into consideration the fact that
     C. seeing as how
     D. for

19.____

20. A. NO CHANGE   B. (Place after *has*)
     C. (Place after *so*)   D. (Place after *visited*

20.____

21. A. NO CHANGE   B. Moreover, tsunamis
     C. However, tsunamis   D. Because tsunamis

21.____

22. A. NO CHANGE   B. 1896 and killed 27,000 people
     C. 1896 and killing 27,000 people   D. 1896, and 27,000 people as well

22.____

Questions 23-33.

DIRECTIONS: Questions 23 through 33 are based on the following passage.

I was <u>married one</u> August on a farm in Maine. The <u>ceremony, itself, taking</u> place in an
        23   24
arbor of pine boughs <u>we had built and constructed</u> in the yard next to the house. On the morning
                 25
of the wedding day, we parked the tractors behind the shed, <u>have tied</u> the dogs to an oak tree to
                                       26
keep them from chasing the guests, and put the cows out to pasture. <u>Thus</u> we had thought of
                                               27
everything, it seemed. we had forgotten how interested a cow can be in what is going on

<u>around them.</u> During the ceremony, my sister <u>(who has taken several years of lessons)</u> was to
    28   29
play a flute solo. We were all listening intently when she <u>had began</u> to play. As the first notes
                                              30
reached us, we were surprised to hear a bass line under the flute's treble melody. Looking

146

5 (#1)

around, the source was quickly discovered. There was Star, my pet Guernsey, her head hanging
          31
over the pasture fence, mooing along with the delicate strains of Bach.

Star took our laughter as being like a compliment, and we took her contribution that way,
                           32
too. It was a sign of approval—the kind you would find only at a farm wedding.

23. A. NO CHANGE   B. married, one   23._____
     C. married on an   D. married, in an

24. A. NO CHANGE   B. ceremony itself taking   24._____
     C. ceremony itself took   D. ceremony, itself took

25. A. NO CHANGE   25._____
     B. which had been built and constructed
     C. we had built and constructed it
     D. we had built

26. A. NO CHANGE   B. tie   26._____
     C. tied   D. tying

27. A. NO CHANGE   27._____
     B. (Do NOT begin new paragraph) And
     C. (Begin new paragraph) But
     D. (Begin new paragraph (Moreover,

28. A. NO CHANGE   B. around her   28._____
     C. in her own vicinity   D. in their immediate area

29. A. NO CHANGE   29._____
     B. (whom has taken many years of lessons)
     C. (who has been trained in music)
     D. OMIT the underlined portion

30. A. NO CHANGE   B. begun   30._____
     C. began   D. would begin

31. A. NO CHANGE   31._____
     B. the discovery of the source was quick
     C. the discovery of the source was quickly made.
     D. we quickly discovered the source.

32. A. NO CHANGE   A. as   32._____
     C. just as   D. as if

6 (#1)

33. A. NO CHANGE   B Yet it was   33.____
    C. But it was   D. Being

Questions 34-42.

DIRECTIONS: Questions 34 through 42 are based on the following passage,

Riding a bicycle in Great Britain is not the same as riding a bicycle in the United States.

Americans bicycling in Britain will find some <u>basic fundamental</u> differences in the rules of the
                                                        34
road and in the attitudes of motorists.

<u>Probably</u> most difficult for the American cyclist is adjusting <u>with</u> British traffic patterns.
    35   36
<u>Knowing that traffic</u> in Britain moves on the left-hand side of the road, bicycling <u>once</u> there is the
    37   38
mirror image of what it is in the United States.

The problem of adjusting to traffic patterns is somewhat lessened, <u>however</u> by the respect
                                                                        39
with which British motorists treat bicyclists. A cyclist in a traffic circle, for example, is given the

same right-of-way <u>with</u> the driver of any other vehicle. However, the cyclist is expected to obey
                    40
the rules of the road. <u>This difference in the American and British attitudes toward bicyclists</u> may
                                                        41
stem from differing attitudes toward the bicycle itself. Whereas Americans frequently view

bicycles as <u>toys, but</u> the British treat them primarily as vehicles.
              42

34. A. NO CHANGE   B basic and fundamental   34.____
    C. basically fundamental   D. basic

35. A. NO CHANGE   B. Even so, probably   35.____
    C. Therefore, probably   D. As a result, probably

36. A. NO CHANGE   B. upon   36.____
    C. on   D. to

37. A. NO CHANGE   B. Seeing that traffic   37.____
    C. Because traffic   D. Traffic

38. A. NO CHANGE   B. once you are   38.____
    C. once one is   D. OMIT the underlined portion

148

7 (#1)

39. A. NO CHANGE   B. also,   39.____
    C. moreover,   D. therefore,

40. A. NO CHANGE   B. as   40.____
    C. as if   D. as with

41. A. NO CHANGE   41.____
    B. difference in the American and British attitudes toward bicyclists
    C. difference, in the American and British attitudes toward bicyclists
    D. difference in the American, and British, attitudes toward bicyclists

42. A. NO CHANGE   B. toy;   42.____
    C. toys,   D. toys; but

Questions 43-51.

DIRECTIONS: Questions 43 through 51 are based on the following passage.

People have always believed that supernatural powers <u>tend toward some influence on</u>
43
lives for good or for ill. Superstition originated with the idea that individuals <u>could in turn,</u> exert
44
influence <u>at</u> spirits. Certain superstitions are <u>so deeply embedded</u> in our culture that intelligent
45   46
people sometimes act in accordance with them.

One common superstitious act is knocking on wood after boasting of good fortune. People once believed that gods inhabited trees and, therefore, were present in the wood used to build houses. Fearing that speaking of good luck within the gods' hearing might anger <u>them, people</u>
47
knocked on wood to deafen the gods and avoid their displeasure.

Another superstitious <u>custom and practice</u> is throwing salt over the left shoulder.
48
<u>Considering</u> salt was once considered sacred, people thought that spilling it brought bad
49
luck. Since right and left represented good and evil, the believers used their right hands, which symbolized good, to throw a pinch of salt over their left shoulders into the eyes of the evil gods.

<u>Because of this</u>, people attempted to avert misfortune.
50
Without realizing the origin of superstitions, many people exhibit superstitious behavior.

<u>Others avoid</u> walking under ladders and stepping on cracks in sidewalks, without having any
51
idea why they are doing so.

149

8 (#1)

43. A. NO CHANGE C. can influence 43.____
    C. tend to influence on D. are having some influence on

44. A. NO CHANGE. B. could, turning 44.____
    C. could, in turn D. could, in turn,

45. A. NO CHANGE C. of 45.____
    C. toward D. on

46. A. NO CHANGE B. deepest embedded 46.____
    C. deepest embedded D. embedded deepest

47. A. NO CHANGE B. them; some people 47.____
    C. them: some people D. them, they

48. A. NO CHANGE B. Custom 48.____
    C traditional custom D. customary habit

49. A. NO CHANGE B. Although 49.____
    C. Because D. Keeping in mind that

50. A. NO CHANGE B. As a result of this, 50.____
    C. Consequently D. In this way,

51. A. NO CHANGE B. Often avoiding 51.____
    C. Avoiding D. They avoid

Questions 52-66.

DIRECTIONS: Questions 52 through 65 are based on the following passage.

In the 1920s, the Y.M.C.A. sponsored one of the first programs <u>in order to promote</u>
                                                                    52
more enlightened public opinion on racial matters; the organization started special university

classes <u>in which</u> young people could study race relations. Among the guest speakers invited to
         53
conduct the sessions, one of the most popular was George Washington Carver, the scientist

from Tuskegee Institute.

As a student, Carver himself had been active in the Y.M.C.A. <u>He shared</u> its evangelical
                                                                54
and educational philosophy. However, in <u>1923,</u> the Y.M.C.A. arranged <u>Carver's first initial</u>
                                           55   56
speaking tour, the scientist accepted with apprehension. He was to speak at several white

colleges, most of whose students had never seen, let alone heard, an educated black man.

150

9 (#1)

Although Carver's appearances <u>did sometimes</u> cause occasional <u>controversy, but</u>
57   58
his quiet dedication prevailed, and his humor quickly won over his audiences. <u>Nevertheless, for</u>
59
the next decade, Carver toured the Northeast, Midwest, and South under Y.M.C.A.

<u>sponsorship. Speaking</u> at places never before open to blacks. On these tours Carver
60
befriended thousands of students, many of <u>whom</u> subsequently corresponded with his
61
<u>afterwards</u>. The <u>tours, unfortunately were</u> not without discomfort for Carver. There were
62   63
the indignities of *Jim Crow* accommodations and racial insults from strangers. <u>As a result,</u>
64
the scientist's enthusiasm never faltered. <u>Avoiding any discussion of</u> the political and social
65
aspects of racial injustice; instead, Carver conducted his whole life as an indirect attack <u>to</u>
66
prejudice. This, as much as his science, is his legacy to humankind.

52. A. NO CHANGE   to promote   52.____
    C. for the promoting of what is   D. for the promotion of what are

53. A. NO CHANGE   C. from which   53.____
    C. that   D. by which

54. A. NO CHANGE   B. Sharing.   54.____
    C. Having Shared   D. Because He Shared

55. A. NO CHANGE   B. 1923   55.____
    C. 1923, and   D. 1923, when

56. A. NO CHANGE   B. Carvers' first, initial   56.____
    C. Carvers first initial   D. Carver's first

57. A. NO CHANGE   B. sometimes did   57.____
    C. did   D. OMIT the underlined portion

58. A. NO CHANGE   B. controversy and   58.____
    C. controversy   D. controversy, however

59. A. NO CHANGE   B. However, for   59.____
    C. However, from   D. For

60. A. NO CHANGE   B. sponsorship and spoke   60.____
    C. sponsorship; and spoke   D. sponsorship, and speaking

10 (#1)

61. A. NO CHANGE
    C. them
    B. who
    D. those
    61.____

62. A. NO CHANGE
    B. later
    C. sometimes later.
    D. OMIT the underlined portion and end the sentence with a period
    62.____

63. A. NO CHANGE
    C. tours unfortunately, were
    B. tours, unfortunately, were
    D. tours, unfortunately, are
    63.____

64. A. NO CHANGE
    C. But
    B. So
    D. Therefore,
    64.____

65. A. NO CHANGE
    C. Having avoided discussing
    B. He avoided discussing
    D. Upon avoiding the discussion of
    65.____

66. A. NO CHANGE
    C. on
    B. over
    D. of
    66.____

Questions 67-75.

DIRECTIONS: Questions 67 through 75 are based on the following passage.

Shooting rapids is not the only way to experience the thrill of canoeing. An ordinary-
                                                                          67
looking stream, innocent of rocks and white water, can provide adventure, as long as it has

three essential features; a swift current, close banks, and has plenty of twists and turns.
                      68   69
A powerful current causes tension, for canoeists know they will have only seconds for
70
executing the maneuvers necessary to prevent crashing into the threes lining the narrow

streams banks. Of course, the narrowness, itself, being crucial in creating the tension. On a
   71   72
broad stream, canoeists can pause frequently, catch their breath, and get their bearings.

However to a narrow stream, where every minute you run the risk of being knocked down by a
        73   74
low-hanging tree limb, they be constantly alert. Yet even the fast current and close banks would

be manageable if the stream were fairly straight. The expenditure of energy required to paddle

furiously, first on one side of the canoe and then on the other, wearies both the nerves as well
                                                                         75
as the body.

11 (#1)

67. A. NO CHANGE B. They say that for adventure an 67.____
     C. Many finding that an D. The old saying that an

68. A. NO CHANGE B. features 68.____
     C. features, D. features; these being

69. A. NO CHANGE B. there must be 69.____
     C. with D. OMIT the underlined portion

70. A. NO CHANGE B. Thus, a 70.____
     C. Therefore, a D. Furthermore, a

71. A. NO CHANGE B. stream's banks. 71.____
     C. streams bank's D. banks of the streams

72. A. NO CHANGE B. narrowness, itself is 72.____
     C. narrowness itself is D. narrowness in itself being

73. A. NO CHANGE B. near 73.____
     C. on D. with

74. A. NO CHANGE B. the canoer runs 74.____
     C. one runs D. they run

75. A. NO CHANGE 75.____
     B. the nerves as well as the body
     C. the nerves, also, as well as the body
     D. not only the body but also the nerves as well

12 (#1)

KEY (CORRECT ANSWERS)

1.	C	21.	A	41.	A	61.	A
2.	A	22.	B	42.	C	62.	D
3.	D	23.	A	43.	B	63.	B
4.	A	24.	C	44.	C	64.	C
5.	B	25.	D	45.	D	65.	B
6.	B	26.	C	46.	A	66.	C
7.	D	27.	C	47.	A	67.	A
8.	B	28.	B	48.	B	68.	B
9.	C	29.	D	49.	C	69.	D
10.	D	30.	C	50.	D	70.	A
11.	A	31.	D	51.	D	71.	B
12.	A	32.	B	52.	B	72.	C
13.	B	33.	A	53.	A	73.	C
14.	C	34.	D	54.	A	74.	D
15.	C	35.	A	55.	D	75.	B
16.	A	36.	D	56.	D		
17.	C	37.	C	57.	C		
18.	D	38.	D	58.	C		
19.	D	39.	A	59.	D		
20.	C	40.	B	60.	B		

PHILOSOPHY, PRINCIPLES, PRACTICES, AND TECHNICS
OF
SUPERVISION, ADMINISTRATION, MANAGEMENT, AND ORGANIZATION

TABLE OF CONTENTS

	Page
MEANING OF SUPERVISION	1
THE OLD AND THE NEW SUPERVISION	1
THE EIGHT (8) BASIC PRINCIPLES OF THE NEW SUPERVISION	1
I. Principle of Responsibility	1
II. Principle of Authority	2
III. Principle of Self-Growth	2
IV. Principle of Individual Worth	2
V. Principle of Creative Leadership	2
VI. Principle of Success and Failure	2
VII. Principle of Science	3
VIII. Principle of Cooperation	3
WHAT IS ADMINISTRATION?	3
I. Practices Commonly Classed as "Supervisory"	3
II. Practices Commonly Classed as "Administrative"	3
III. Practices Commonly Classed as Both "Supervisory" and "Administrative"	4
RESPONSIBILITIES OF THE SUPERVISOR	4
COMPETENCIES OF THE SUPERVISOR	4
THE PROFESSIONAL SUPERVISOR-EMPLOYEE RELATIONSHIP	4
MINI-TEXT IN SUPERVISION, ADMINISTRATION, MANAGEMENT, AND ORGANIZATION	5
I. Brief Highlights	5
A. Levels of Management	6
B. What the Supervisor Must Learn	6
C. A Definition of Supervision	6
D. Elements of the Team Concept	6
E. Principles of Organization	6
F. The Four Important Parts of Every Job	7
G. Principles of Delegation	7
H. Principles of Effective Communications	7
I. Principles of Work Improvement	7
J. Areas of Job Improvement	7
K. Seven Key Points in Making Improvements	8

L.	Corrective Techniques for Job Improvement	8
M.	A Planning Checklist	8
N.	Five Characteristics of Good Directions	9
O.	Types of Directions	9
P.	Controls	9
Q.	Orienting the New Employee	9
R.	Checklist for Orienting New Employees	9
S.	Principles of Learning	10
T.	Causes of Poor Performance	10
U.	Four Major Steps in On-the-Job Instructions	10
V.	Employees Want Five Things	10
W.	Some Don'ts in Regard to Praise	11
X.	How to Gain Your Workers' Confidence	11
Y.	Sources of Employee Problems	11
Z.	The Supervisor's Key to Discipline	11
AA.	Five Important Processes of Management	12
BB.	When the Supervisor Fails to Plan	12
CC.	Fourteen General Principles of Management	12
DD.	Change	12

II.	Brief Topical Summaries	13
A.	Who/What is the Supervisor?	13
B.	The Sociology of Work	13
C.	Principles and Practices of Supervision	14
D.	Dynamic Leadership	14
E.	Processes for Solving Problems	15
F.	Training for Results	15
G.	Health, Safety, and Accident Prevention	16
H.	Equal Employment Opportunity	16
I.	Improving Communications	16
J.	Self-Development	17
K.	Teaching and Training	17
	1. The Teaching Process	17
	a. Preparation	17
	b. Presentation	18
	c. Summary	18
	d. Application	18
	e. Evaluation	18
	2. Teaching Methods	18
	a. Lecture	18
	b. Discussion	18
	c. Demonstration	19
	d. Performance	19
	e. Which Method to Use	19

PHILOSOPHY, PRINCIPLES, PRACTICES, AND TECHNICS
OF
SUPERVISION, ADMINISTRATION, MANAGEMENT, AND ORGANIZATION

MEANING OF SUPERVISION

The extension of the democratic philosophy has been accompanied by an extension in the scope of supervision. Modern leaders and supervisors no longer think of supervision in the narrow sense of being confined chiefly to visiting employees, supplying materials, or rating the staff. They regard supervision as being intimately related to all the concerned agencies of society, they speak of the supervisor's function in terms of "growth," rather than the "improvement" of employees.

This modern concept of supervision may be defined as follows: Supervision is leadership and the development of leadership within groups which are cooperatively engaged in inspection, research, training, guidance, and evaluation.

THE OLD AND THE NEW SUPERVISION

TRADITIONAL
1. Inspection
2. Focused on the employee
3. Visitation
4. Random and haphazard
5. Imposed and authoritarian
6. One person usually

MODERN
1. Study and analysis
2. Focused on aims, materials, methods, supervisors, employees, environment
3. Demonstrations, intervisitation, workshops, directed reading, bulletins, etc.
4. Definitely organized and planned (scientific)
5. Cooperative and democratic
6. Many persons involved (creative)

THE EIGHT (8) BASIC PRINCIPLES OF THE NEW SUPERVISION

I. Principle of Responsibility
   Authority to act and responsibility for acting must be joined.
   A. If you give responsibility, give authority.
   B. Define employee duties clearly.
   C. Protect employees from criticism by others.
   D. Recognize the rights as well as obligations of employees.
   E. Achieve the aims of a democratic society insofar as it is possible within the area of your work.
   F. Establish a situation favorable to training and learning.
   G. Accept ultimate responsibility for everything done in your section, unit, office, division, department.
   H. Good administration and good supervision are inseparable.

II. Principle of Authority

The success of the supervisor is measured by the extent to which the power of authority is not used.

A. Exercise simplicity and informality in supervision
B. Use the simplest machinery of supervision
C. If it is good for the organization as a whole, it is probably justified.
D. Seldom be arbitrary or authoritative.
E. Do not base your work on the power of position or of personality.
F. Permit and encourage the free expression of opinions.

III. Principle of Self-Growth

The success of the supervisor is measured by the extent to which, and the speed with which, he is no longer needed.

A. Base criticism on principles, not on specifics.
B. Point out higher activities to employees.
C. Train for self-thinking by employees to meet new situations.
D. Stimulate initiative, self-reliance, and individual responsibility
E. Concentrate on stimulating the growth of employees rather than on removing defects.

IV. Principle of Individual Worth

Respect for the individual is a paramount consideration in supervision.

A. Be human and sympathetic in dealing with employees.
B. Don't nag about things to be done.
C. Recognize the individual differences among employees and seek opportunities to permit best expression of each personality.

V. Principle of Creative Leadership

The best supervision is that which is not apparent to the employee.

A. Stimulate, don't drive employees to creative action.
B. Emphasize doing good things.
C. Encourage employees to do what they do best.
D. Do not be too greatly concerned with details of subject or method.
E. Do not be concerned exclusively with immediate problems and activities.
F. Reveal higher activities and make them both desired and maximally possible.
G. Determine procedures in the light of each situation but see that these are derived from a sound basic philosophy.
H. Aid, inspire, and lead so as to liberate the creative spirit latent in all good employees.

VI. Principle of Success and Failure

There are no unsuccessful employees, only unsuccessful supervisors who have failed to give proper leadership.

A. Adapt suggestions to the capacities, attitudes, and prejudices of employees.
B. Be gradual, be progressive, be persistent.
C. Help the employee find the general principle; have the employee apply his own problem to the general principle.
D. Give adequate appreciation for good work and honest effort.
E. Anticipate employee difficulties and help to prevent them.
F. Encourage employees to do the desirable things they will do anyway.
G. Judge your supervision by the results it secures.

3

VII. Principle of Science
Successful supervision is scientific, objective, and experimental. It is based on facts, not on prejudices.
A. Be cumulative in results.
B. Never divorce your suggestions from the goals of training.
C. Don't be impatient of results.
D. Keep all matters on a professional, not a personal, level.
E. Do not be concerned exclusively with immediate problems and activities.
F. Use objective means of determining achievement and rating where possible.

VIII. Principle of Cooperation
Supervision is a cooperative enterprise between supervisor and employee.
A. Begin with conditions as they are.
B. Ask opinions of all involved when formulating policies.
C. Organization is as good as its weakest link.
D. Let employees help to determine policies and department programs.
E. Be approachable and accessible—physically and mentally.
F. Develop pleasant social relationships.

WHAT IS ADMINISTRATION

Administration is concerned with providing the environment, the material facilities, and the operational procedures that will promote the maximum growth and development of supervisors and employees. (Organization is an aspect and a concomitant of administration.)

There is no sharp line of demarcation between supervision and administration; these functions are intimately interrelated and, often, overlapping. They are complementary activities.

I. Practices Commonly Classed as "Supervisory"
A. Conducting employees' conferences
B. Visiting sections, units, offices, divisions, departments
C. Arranging for demonstrations
D. Examining plans
E. Suggesting professional reading
F. Interpreting bulletins
G. Recommending in-service training courses
H. Encouraging experimentation
I. Appraising employee morale
J. Providing for intervisitation

II. Practices Commonly Classified as "Administrative"
A. Management of the office
B. Arrangement of schedules for extra duties
C. Assignment of rooms or areas
D. Distribution of supplies
E. Keeping records and reports
F. Care of audio-visual materials
G. Keeping inventory records
H. Checking record cards and books

4

 I. Programming special activities
 J. Checking on the attendance and punctuality of employees

III. Practices Commonly Classified as Both "Supervisory" and "Administrative"
 A. Program construction
 B. Testing or evaluating outcomes
 C. Personnel accounting
 D. Ordering instructional materials

RESPONSIBILITIES OF THE SUPERVISOR

A person employed in a supervisory capacity must constantly be able to improve his own efficiency and ability. He represent the employer to the employees and only continuous self-examination can make him a capable supervisor.

Leadership and training are the supervisor's responsibility. An efficient working unit is one in which the employees work with the supervisor. It is his job to bring out the best in his employees. He must always be relaxed, courteous, and calm in his association with his employees. Their feelings are important, and a harsh attitude does not develop the most efficient employees.

COMPETENCES OF THE SUPERVISOR

 I. Complete knowledge of the duties and responsibilities of his position.
 II. To be able to organize a job, plan ahead, and carry through.
 III. To have self-confidence and initiative.
 IV. To be able to handle the unexpected situation and make quick decisions.
 V. To be able to properly train subordinates in the positions they are best suited for.
 VI. To be able to keep good human relations among his subordinates.
 VII. To be able to keep good human relations between his subordinates and himself and to earn their respect and trust.

THE PROFESSIONAL SUPERVISOR-EMPLOYEE RELATIONSHIP

There are two kinds of efficiency: one kind is only apparent and is produced in organizations through the exercise of mere discipline; this is but a simulation of the second, or true, efficiency which springs from spontaneous cooperation. If you are a manager, no matter how great or small your responsibility, it is your job, in the final analysis, to create and develop this involuntary cooperation among the people whom you supervise. For, no matter how powerful a combination of money, machines, and materials a company may have, this is a dead and sterile thing without a team of willing, thinking, and articulate people to guide it.

The following 21 points are presented as indicative of the exemplary basic relationship that should exist between supervisor and employee:

1. Each person wants to be liked and respected by his fellow employee and wants to be treated with consideration and respect by his superior.
2. The most competent employee will make an error. However, in a unit where good relations exist between the supervisor and his employees, tenseness and fear do not exist. Thus, errors are not hidden or covered up, and the efficiency of a unit is not impaired.

3. Subordinates resent rules, regulations, or orders that are unreasonable or unexplained.
4. Subordinates are quick to resent unfairness, harshness, injustices, and favoritism.
5. An employee will accept responsibility if he knows that he will be complimented for a job well done, and not too harshly chastised for failure; that his supervisor will check the cause of the failure, and, if it was the supervisor's fault, he will assume the blame therefore. If it was the employee's fault, his supervisor will explain the correct method or means of handling the responsibility.
6. An employee wants to receive credit for a suggestion he has made, that is used. If a suggestion cannot be used, the employee is entitled to an explanation. The supervisor should not say "no" and close the subject.
7. Fear and worry slow up a worker's ability. Poor working environment can impair his physical and mental health. A good supervisor avoids forceful methods, threats, and arguments to get a job done.
8. A forceful supervisor is able to train his employees individually and as a team, and is able to motivate them in the proper channels.
9. A mature supervisor is able to properly evaluate his subordinates and to keep them happy and satisfied.
10. A sensitive supervisor will never patronize his subordinates.
11. A worthy supervisor will respect his employees' confidences.
12. Definite and clear-cut responsibilities should be assigned to each executive.
13. Responsibility should always be coupled with corresponding authority.
14. No change should be made in the scope or responsibilities of a position without a definite understanding to that effect on the part of all persons concerned.
15. No executive or employee, occupying a single position in the organization, should be subject to definite orders from more than one source.
16. Orders should never be given to subordinates over the head of a responsible executive. Rather than do this, the officer in question should be supplanted.
17. Criticisms of subordinates should, whoever possible, be made privately, and in no case should a subordinate be criticized in the presence of executives or employees of equal or lower rank.
18. No dispute or difference between executives or employees as to authority or responsibilities should be considered too trivial for prompt and careful adjudication.
19. Promotions, wage changes, and disciplinary action should always be approved by the executive immediately superior to the one directly responsible.
20. No executive or employee should ever be required, or expected, to be at the same time an assistant to, and critic of, another.
21. Any executive whose work is subject to regular inspection should, wherever practicable, be given the assistance and facilities necessary to enable him to maintain an independent check of the quality of his work.

MINI-TEXT IN SUPERVISION, ADMINISTRATION, MANAGEMENT, AND ORGANIZATION

I. Brief Highlights

Listed concisely and sequentially are major headings and important data in the field for quick recall and review.

A. Levels of Management
Any organization of some size has several levels of management. In terms of a ladder, the levels are:

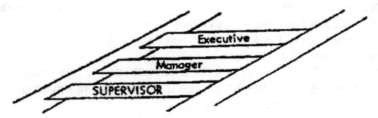

The first level is very important because it is the beginning point of management leadership.

B. What the Supervisor Must Learn
A supervisor must learn to:
1. Deal with people and their differences
2. Get the job done through people
3. Recognize the problems when they exist
4. Overcome obstacles to good performance
5. Evaluate the performance of people
6. Check his own performance in terms of accomplishment

C. A Definition of Supervisor
The term supervisor means any individual having authority, in the interests of the employer, to hire, transfer, suspend, lay-off, recall, promote, discharge, assign, reward, or discipline other employees or responsibility to direct them, or to adjust their grievances, or effectively to recommend such action, if, in connection with the foregoing, exercise of such authority is not of a merely routine or clerical nature but requires the use of independent judgment.

D. Elements of the Team Concept
What is involved in teamwork? The component parts are:
1. Members
2. A leader
3. Goals
4. Plans
5. Cooperation
6. Spirit

E. Principles of Organization
1. A team member must know what his job is.
2. Be sure that the nature and scope of a job are understood.
3. Authority and responsibility should be carefully spelled out.
4. A supervisor should be permitted to make the maximum number of decisions affecting his employees.
5. Employees should report to only one supervisor.
6. A supervisor should direct only as many employees as he can handle effectively.
7. An organization plan should be flexible.

7

8. Inspection and performance of work should be separate.
9. Organizational problems should receive immediate attention.
10. Assign work in line with ability and experience.

F. The Four Important Parts of Every Job
1. Inherent in every job is the *accountability* for results.
2. A second set of factors in every job is *responsibilities*.
3. Along with duties and responsibilities one must have the *authority* to act within certain limits without obtaining permission to proceed.
4. No job exists in a vacuum. The supervisor is surrounded by key *relationships*.

G. Principles of Delegation
Where work is delegated for the first time, the supervisor should think in terms of these questions:
1. Who is best qualified to do this?
2. Can an employee improve his abilities by doing this?
3. How long should an employee spend on this?
4. Are there any special problems for which he will need guidance?
5. How broad a delegation can I make?

H. Principles of Effective Communications
1. Determine the media.
2. To whom directed?
3. Identification and source authority.
4. Is communication understood?

I. Principles of Work Improvement
1. Most people usually do only the work which is assigned to them.
2. Workers are likely to fit assigned work into the time available to perform it.
3. A good workload usually stimulates output.
4. People usually do their best work when they know that results will be reviewed or inspected.
5. Employees usually feel that someone else is responsible for conditions of work, workplace layout, job methods, type of tools/equipment, and other such factors.
6. Employees are usually defensive about their job security.
7. Employees have natural resistance to change.
8. Employees can support or destroy a supervisor.
9. A supervisor usually earns the respect of his people through his personal example of diligence and efficiency.

J. Areas of Job Improvement
The areas of job improvement are quite numerous, but the most common ones which a supervisor can identify and utilize are:
1. Departmental layout
2. Flow of work
3. Workplace layout
4. Utilization of manpower
5. Work methods
6. Materials handling

8

K. Seven Key Points in Making Improvements
1. Select the job to be improved
2. Study how it is being done now
3. Question the present method
4. Determine actions to be taken
5. Chart proposed method
6. Get approval and apply
7. Solicit worker participation

L. Corrective Techniques of Job Improvement
Specific Problems
1. Size of workload
2. Inability to meet schedules
3. Strain and fatigue
4. Improper use of men and skills
5. Waste, poor quality, unsafe conditions
6. Bottleneck conditions that hinder output
7. Poor utilization of equipment and machine
8. Efficiency and productivity of labor

General Improvement
1. Departmental layout
2. Flow of work
3. Work plan layout
4. Utilization of manpower
5. Work methods
6. Materials handling
7. Utilization of equipment
8. Motion economy

Corrective Techniques
1. Study with scale model
2. Flow chart study
3. Motion analysis
4. Comparison of units produced to standard allowance
5. Methods analysis
6. Flow chart and equipment study
7. Down time vs. running time
8. Motion analysis

M. A Planning Checklist
1. Objectives
2. Controls
3. Delegations
4. Communications
5. Resources
6. Manpower

164

9

7. Equipment
8. Supplies and materials
9. Utilization of time
10. Safety
11. Money
12. Work
13. Timing of improvements

N. Five Characteristics of Good Directions
In order to get results, directions must be:
1. Possible of accomplishment
2. Agreeable with worker interests
3. Related to mission
4. Planned and complete
5. Unmistakably clear

O. Types of Directions
1. Demands or direct orders
2. Requests
3. Suggestion or implication
4. volunteering

P. Controls
A typical listing of the overall areas in which the supervisor should establish controls might be:
1. Manpower
2. Materials
3. Quality of work
4. Quantity of work
5. Time
6. Space
7. Money
8. Methods

Q. Orienting the New Employee
1. Prepare for him
2. Welcome the new employee
3. Orientation for the job
4. Follow-up

R. Checklist for Orienting New Employees   Yes   No
1. Do you appreciate the feelings of new employees when they first report for work?   ___   ___
2. Are you aware of the fact that the new employee must make a big adjustment to his job?   ___   ___
3. Have you given him good reasons for liking the job and the organization?   ___   ___
4. Have you prepared for his first day on the job?   ___   ___
5. Did you welcome him cordially and make him feel needed?   ___   ___

165

10

	Yes	No

6. Did you establish rapport with him so that he feels free to talk and discuss matters with you? ____ ____

7. Did you explain his job to him and his relationship to you? ____ ____

8. Does he know that his work will be evaluated periodically on a basis that is fair and objective? ____ ____

9. Did you introduce him to his fellow workers in such a way that they are likely to accept him? ____ ____

10. Does he know what employee benefits he will receive? ____ ____

11. Does he understand the importance of being on the job and what to do if he must leave his duty station? ____ ____

12. Has he been impressed with the importance of accident prevention and safe practice? ____ ____

13. Does he generally know his way around the department? ____ ____

14. Is he under the guidance of a sponsor who will teach the right way of doing things? ____ ____

15. Do you plan to follow-up so that he will continue to adjust successfully to his job? ____ ____

S. Principles of Learning
1. Motivation
2. Demonstration or explanation
3. Practice

T. Causes of Poor Performance
1. Improper training for job
2. Wrong tools
3. Inadequate directions
4. Lack of supervisory follow-up
5. Poor communications
6. Lack of standards of performance
7. Wrong work habits
8. Low morale
9. Other

U. Four Major Steps in On-The-Job Instruction
1. Prepare the worker
2. Present the operation
3. Tryout performance
4. Follow-up

V. Employees Want Five Things
1. Security
2. Opportunity
3. Recognition
4. Inclusion
5. Expression

11

W. Some Don'ts in Regard to Praise
1. Don't praise a person for something he hasn't done.
2. Don't praise a person unless you can be sincere.
3. Don't be sparing in praise just because your superior withholds it from you.
4. Don't let too much time elapse between good performance and recognition of it

X. How to Gain Your Workers' Confidence
Methods of developing confidence include such things as:
1. Knowing the interests, habits, hobbies of employees
2. Admitting your own inadequacies
3. Sharing and telling of confidence in others
4. Supporting people when they are in trouble
5. Delegating matters that can be well handled
6. Being frank and straightforward about problems and working conditions
7. Encouraging others to bring their problems to you
8. Taking action on problems which impede worker progress

Y. Sources of Employee Problems
On-the-job causes might be such things as:
1. A feeling that favoritism is exercised in assignments
2. Assignment of overtime
3. An undue amount of supervision
4. Changing methods or systems
5. Stealing of ideas or trade secrets
6. Lack of interest in job
7. Threat of reduction in force
8. Ignorance or lack of communications
9. Poor equipment
10. Lack of knowing how supervisor feels toward employee
11. Shift assignments

Off-the-job problems might have to do with:
1. Health
2. Finances
3. Housing
4. Family

Z. The Supervisor's Key to Discipline
There are several key points about discipline which the supervisor should keep in mind:
1. Job discipline is one of the disciplines of life and is directed by the supervisor.
2. It is more important to correct an employee fault than to fix blame for it.
3. Employee performance is affected by problems both on the job and off.
4. Sudden or abrupt changes in behavior can be indications of important employee problems.
5. Problems should be dealt with as soon as possible after they are identified.
6. The attitude of the supervisor may have more to do with solving problems than the techniques of problem solving.
7. Correction of employee behavior should be resorted to only after the supervisor is sure that training or counseling will not be helpful.

12

8. Be sure to document your disciplinary actions.
9. Make sure that you are disciplining on the basis of facts rather than personal feelings.
10. Take each disciplinary step in order, being careful not to make snap judgments, or decisions based on impatience.

AA. Five Important Processes of Management
1. Planning
2. Organizing
3. Scheduling
4. Controlling
5. Motivating

BB. When the Supervisor Fails to Plan
1. Supervisor creates impression of not knowing his job
2. May lead to excessive overtime
3. Job runs itself—supervisor lacks control
4. Deadlines and appointments missed
5. Parts of the work go undone
6. Work interrupted by emergencies
7. Sets a bad example
8. Uneven workload creates peaks and valleys
9. Too much time on minor details at expense of more important tasks

CC. Fourteen General Principles of Management
1. Division of work
2. Authority and responsibility
3. Discipline
4. Unity of command
5. Unity of direction
6. Subordination of individual interest to general interest
7. Remuneration of personnel
8. Centralization
9. Scalar chain
10. Order
11. Equity
12. Stability of tenure of personnel
13. Initiative
14. Esprit de corps

DD. Change

Bringing about change is perhaps attempted more often, and yet less well understood, than anything else the supervisor does. How do people generally react to change? (People tend to resist change that is imposed upon them by other individuals or circumstances.

Change is characteristic of every situation. It is a part of every real endeavor where the efforts of people are concerned.

168

13

1. Why do people resist change?
   People may resist change because of:
   a. Fear of the unknown
   b. Implied criticism
   c. Unpleasant experiences in the past
   d. Fear of loss of status
   e. Threat to the ego
   f. Fear of loss of economic stability

2. How can we best overcome the resistance to change?
   In initiating change, take these steps:
   a. Get ready to sell
   b. Identify sources of help
   c. Anticipate objections
   d. Sell benefits
   e. Listen in depth
   f. Follow up

II. Brief Topical Summaries

A. Who/What is the Supervisor?
   1. The supervisor is often called the "highest level employee and the lowest level manager."
   2. A supervisor is a member of both management and the work group. He acts as a bridge between the two.
   3. Most problems in supervision are in the area of human relations, or people problems.
   4. Employees expect: Respect, opportunity to learn and to advance, and a sense of belonging, and so forth.
   5. Supervisors are responsible for directing people and organizing work. Planning is of paramount importance.
   6. A position description is a set of duties and responsibilities inherent to a given position.
   7. It is important to keep the position description up-to-date and to provide each employee with his own copy.

B. The Sociology of Work
   1. People are alike in many ways; however, each individual is unique.
   2. The supervisor is challenged in getting to know employee differences. Acquiring skills in evaluating individuals is an asset.
   3. Maintaining meaningful working relationships in the organization is of great importance.
   4. The supervisor has an obligation to help individuals to develop to their fullest potential.
   5. Job rotation on a planned basis helps to build versatility and to maintain interest and enthusiasm in work groups.
   6. Cross training (job rotation) provides backup skills.

169

14

7. The supervisor can help reduce tension by maintaining a sense of humor, providing guidance to employees, and by making reasonable and timely decisions. Employees respond favorably to working under reasonably predictable circumstances.
8. Change is characteristic of all managerial behavior. The supervisor must adjust to changes in procedures, new methods, technological changes, and to a number of new and sometimes challenging situations.
9. To overcome the natural tendency for people to resist change, the supervisor should become more skillful in initiating change.

C. Principles and Practices of Supervision
   1. Employees should be required to answer to only one superior.
   2. A supervisor can effectively direct only a limited number of employees, depending upon the complexity, variety, and proximity of the jobs involved.
   3. The organizational chart presents the organization in graphic form. It reflects lines of authority and responsibility as well as interrelationships of units within the organization.
   4. Distribution of work can be improved through an analysis using the "Work Distribution Chart."
   5. The "Work Distribution Chart" reflects the division of work within a unit in understandable form.
   6. When related tasks are given to an employee, he has a better chance of increasing his skills through training.
   7. The individual who is given the responsibility for tasks must also be given the appropriate authority to insure adequate results.
   8. The supervisor should delegate repetitive, routine work. Preparation of recurring reports, maintaining leave and attendance records are some examples.
   9. Good discipline is essential to good task performance. Discipline is reflected in the actions of employees on the job in the absence of supervision.
   10. Disciplinary action may have to be taken when the positive aspects of discipline have failed. Reprimand, warning, and suspension are examples of disciplinary action.
   11. If a situation calls for a reprimand, be sure it is deserved and remember it is to be done in private.

D. Dynamic Leadership
   1. A style is a personal method or manner of exerting influence.
   2. Authoritarian leaders often see themselves as the source of power and authority.
   3. The democratic leader often perceives the group as the source of authority and power.
   4. Supervisors tend to do better when using the pattern of leadership that is most natural for them.
   5. Social scientists suggest that the effective supervisor use the leadership style that best fits the problem or circumstances involved.
   6. All four styles—telling, selling, consulting, joining—have their place. Using one does not preclude using the other at another time.

15

7. The theory X point of view assumes that the average person dislikes work, will avoid it whenever possible, and must be coerced to achieve organizational objectives.
8. The theory Y point of view assumes that the average person considers work to be a natural as play, and, when the individual is committed, he requires little supervision or direction to accomplish desired objectives.
9. The leader's basic assumptions concerning human behavior and human nature affect his actions, decisions, and other managerial practices.
10. Dissatisfaction among employees is often present, but difficult to isolate. The supervisor should seek to weaken dissatisfaction by keeping promises, being sincere and considerate, keeping employees informed, and so forth.
11. Constructive suggestions should be encouraged during the natural progress of the work.

E. Processes for Solving Problems
1. People find their daily tasks more meaningful and satisfying when they can improve them.
2. The causes of problems, or the key factors, are often hidden in the background. Ability to solve problems often involves the ability to isolate them from their backgrounds. There is some substance to the cliché that some persons "can't see the forest for the trees."
3. New procedures are often developed from old ones. Problems should be broken down into manageable parts. New ideas can be adapted from old one.
4. People think differently in problem-solving situations. Using a logical, patterned approach is often useful. One approach found to be useful includes these steps:
   a. Define the problem
   b. Establish objectives
   c. Get the facts
   d. Weigh and decide
   e. Take action
   f. Evaluate action

F. Training for Results
1. Participants respond best when they feel training is important to them.
2. The supervisor has responsibility for the training and development of those who report to him.
3. When training is delegated to others, great care must be exercised to insure the trainer has knowledge, aptitude, and interest for his work as a trainer.
4. Training (learning) of some type goes on continually. The most successful supervisor makes certain the learning contributes in a productive manner to operational goals.
5. New employees are particularly susceptible to training. Older employees facing new job situations require specific training, as well as having need for development and growth opportunities.
6. Training needs require continuous monitoring.
7. The training officer of an agency is a professional with a responsibility to assist supervisors in solving training problems.

171

16

8. Many of the self-development steps important to the supervisor's own growth are equally important to the development of peers and subordinates. Knowledge of these is important when the supervisor consults with others on development and growth opportunities.

G. Health, Safety, and Accident Prevention
   1. Management-minded supervisors take appropriate measures to assist employees in maintaining health and in assuring safe practices in the work environment.
   2. Effective safety training and practices help to avoid injury and accidents.
   3. Safety should be a management goal. All infractions of safety which are observed should be corrected without exception.
   4. Employees' safety attitude, training and instruction, provision of safe tools and equipment, supervision, and leadership are considered highly important factors which contribute to safety and which can be influenced directly by supervisors.
   5. When accidents do occur, they should be investigated promptly for very important reasons, including the fact that information which is gained can be used to prevent accidents in the future.

H. Equal Employment Opportunity
   1. The supervisor should endeavor to treat all employees fairly, without regard to religion, race, sex, or national origin.
   2. Groups tend to reflect the attitude of the leader. Prejudice can be detected even in very subtle form. Supervisors must strive to create a feeling of mutual respect and confidence in every employee.
   3. Complete utilization of all human resources is a national goal. Equitable consideration should be accorded women in the work force, minority-group members, the physically and mentally handicapped, and the older employee. The important question is: "Who can do the job?"
   4. Training opportunities, recognition for performance, overtime assignments, promotional opportunities, and all other personnel actions are to be handled on an equitable basis.

I. Improving Communications
   1. Communications is achieving understanding between the sender and the receiver of a message. It also means sharing information—the creation of understanding.
   2. Communication is basic to all human activity. Words are means of conveying meanings; however, real meanings are in people.
   3. There are very practical differences in the effectiveness of one-way, impersonal, and two-way communications. Words spoken face-to-face are better understood. Telephone conversations are effective, but lack the rapport of person-to-person exchanges. The whole person communicates.
   4. Cooperation and communication in an organization go hand in hand. When there is a mutual respect between people, spelling out rules and procedures for communicating is unnecessary.
   5. There are several barriers to effective communications. These include failure to listen with respect and understanding, lack of skill in feedback, and misinterpreting the meanings of words used by the speaker. It is also common

17

practice to listen to what we want to hear, and tune out things we do not want to hear.

6. Communication is management's chief problem. The supervisor should accept the challenge to communicate more effectively and to improve interagency and intra-agency communications.

7. The supervisor may often plan for and conduct meetings. The planning phase is critical and may determine the success or the failure of a meeting.

8. Speaking before groups usually requires extra effort. Stage fright may never disappear completely, but it can be controlled.

J. Self-Development
1. Every employee is responsible for his own self-development.
2. Toastmaster and toastmistress clubs offer opportunities to improve skills in oral communications.
3. Planning for one's own self-development is of vital importance. Supervisors know their own strengths and limitations better than anyone else.
4. Many opportunities are open to aid the supervisor in his developmental efforts, including job assignments; training opportunities, both governmental and non-governmental—to include universities and professional conferences and seminars.
5. Programmed instruction offers a means of studying at one's own rate.
6. Where difficulties may arise from a supervisor's being away from his work for training, he may participate in televised home study or correspondence courses to meet his self-development needs.

K. Teaching and Training
1. The Teaching Process
Teaching is encouraging and guiding the learning activities of students toward established goals. In most cases this process consists of five steps: preparation, presentation, summarization, evaluation, and application.

a. Preparation
Preparation is two-fold in nature; that of the supervisor and the employee. Preparation by the supervisor is absolutely essential to success. He must know what, when, where, how, and whom he will teach. Some of the factors that should be considered are:
1) The objectives
2) The materials needed
3) The methods to be used
4) Employee participation
5) Employee interest
6) Training aids
7) Evaluation
8) Summarization

Employee preparation consists in preparing the employee to receive the material. Probably the most important single factor in the preparation of the employee is arousing and maintaining his interest. He must know the objectives of the training, why he is there, how the material can be used, and its importance to him.

18

b. Presentation
In presentation, have a carefully designed plan and follow it. The plan should be accurate and complete, yet flexible enough to meet situations as they arise. The method of presentation will be determined by the particular situation and objectives.

c. Summary
A summary should be made at the end of every training unit and program. In addition, there may be internal summaries depending on the nature of the material being taught. The important thing is that the trainee must always be able to understand how each part of the new material relates to the whole.

d. Application
The supervisor must arrange work so the employee will be given a chance to apply new knowledge or skills while the material is still clear in his mind and interest is high. The trainee does not really know whether he has learned the material until he has been given a chance to apply it. If the material is not applied, it loses most of its value.

e. Evaluation
The purpose of all training is to promote learning. To determine whether the training has been a success or failure, the supervisor must evaluate this learning.
In the broadest sense, evaluation includes all the devices, methods, skills, and techniques used by the supervisor to keep himself and the employees informed as to their progress toward the objectives they are pursuing. The extent to which the employee has mastered the knowledge, skills, and abilities, or changed his attitudes, as determined by the program objectives, is the extent to which instruction has succeeded or failed.
Evaluation should not be confined to the end of the lesson, day, or program but should be used continuously. We shall note later the way this relates to the rest of the teaching process.

2. Teaching Methods
A teaching method is a pattern of identifiable student and instructor activity used in presenting training material.
All supervisors are faced with the problem of deciding which method should be used at a given time.

a. Lecture
The lecture is direct oral presentation of material by the supervisor. The present trend is to place less emphasis on the trainer's activity and more on that of the trainee.

b. Discussion
Teaching by discussion or conference involves using questions and other techniques to arouse interest and focus attention upon certain areas, and by doing so creating a learning situation. This can be one of the most

174

valuable methods because it gives the employees an opportunity to express their ideas and pool their knowledge.

c. Demonstration

The demonstration is used to teach how something works or how to do something. It can be used to show a principle or what the results of a series of actions will be. A well-staged demonstration is particularly effective because it shows proper methods of performance in a realistic manner.

d. Performance

Performance is one of the most fundamental of all learning techniques or teaching methods. The trainee may be able to tell how a specific operation should be performed but he cannot be sure he knows how to perform the operation until he has done so.
As with all methods, there are certain advantages and disadvantages to each method.

e. Which Method to Use

Moreover, there are other methods and techniques of teaching. It is difficult to use any method without other methods entering into it. In any learning situation, a combination of methods is usually more effective than any one method alone.

Finally, evaluation must be integrated into the other aspects of the teaching-learning process.

It must be used in the motivation of the trainees; it must be used to assist in developing understanding during the training; and it must be related to employee application of the results of training.

This is distinctly the role of the supervisor.